# Reference Point

# Reference Point

BY

ARTHUR HOPKINS

AH : RP

Reflections on creative ways in general
with special reference to creative ways
in the theatre.

SAMUEL FRENCH

NEW YORK      HOLLYWOOD

SAMUEL FRENCH Ltd.    LONDON

PRINTED IN THE UNITED STATES OF AMERICA
BY THE VAIL-BALLOU PRESS, INC., BINGHAMTON, N. Y.

TO

ROBERT EDMOND JONES

This book is based on a series of papers on the theatre read by the author at the 1947 Summer Theatre Seminar sponsored by Fordham University for drama teachers, directors and students from all parts of the country.

Following each of the author's papers there was a question period. The pertinent points thus brought out are here condensed, clarified and in some cases amplified.

# CONTENTS

# Reference Point

# HALF-MEN AND WHOLE MEN

IN THE days when the theatre flourished throughout the country and formed a memorable part of the lives of many who were its devotees, the theatre was an end in itself. It was not a means to a desired goal. Being part of it, was the only goal.

Few were foolish enough to believe that the theatre was the road to riches or fame. Yet, intrepid bands of players, year after year, went to big and little communities throughout the land bearing their special brand of benison. There is scarcely a whistle-stop in America where a monument to the unknown actor would not be fitting.

Because of this impractical devotion actors were looked upon as irresponsible meanderers who, for some strange reason, were lovable and to be envied. With no apparent justification they had the joy of living in them and they shared it with others. Wherever encountered, in dirty trains, grubby hotels or dingy restaurants, they were the life of the party.

Equally in the company of local or national celebrities, glittering towers of success, they somehow made those about them seem to shine less brightly.

They brought more than diversion to a community. They left a sense of something lacking in obviously more estimable pursuits.

Occasionally a local boy or girl seeing something more stimulating in life than was to be found in the local scene, managed to run off with a troupe and was mourned as one carried off by the gypsies.

Yet, it was these irresponsibles who took the classics, principally Shakespeare, that earlier runaway profligate, to many who became permanently enriched. They helped make Shakespeare an honored resident in many libraries where the only previous classic had been the Bible. If a home was to have only two classics, no wiser choice could have been made. In them is unsurpassed literary education, sources evident in the unforgettable use of poetic English by Lincoln, and in our day by Winston Churchill.

The great stars of that day were familiars to theatre audiences in all parts of the land. New York was only one of many stands, and by no means the favorite one, not comparable in welcome to San Francisco, New Orleans, Boston, Philadelphia, Chicago and many smaller cities. New York as theatre arbiter had not yet been so honored. The theatre then was national. It was an enriching and essential part of many lives and its memories among the most treasured. It was more than diversion. It was part of the country's culture.

Naturally, in an economy which saw all the answers to mankind's problems in organization, the unorganized ways of the theatre could not escape. And certainly organization was needed if the theatre was to be economically acceptable. But like all organization, it put more valuation on combined strength than on individual effort.

Klaw and Erlanger were the first great organizers. Pursuing organization to its ultimate efficiency, Klaw and Erlanger became a trust. It was here that the centralization of the theatre in New York began.

Klaw and Erlanger did not escape the arrogance that is the canker of power. There is no greater invitation to challenge than arrogance. Three unexpected young men from Syracuse, Sam, Lee and J. J. Shubert, took up the challenge and finally broke the monopoly by beginning another one.

The Shuberts had genius for organization. Surmounting the tragic loss of their leader brother, Lee and J. J. went on to fulfill Sam's dream. Theirs was industry and tenacity that the easy going theatre had never known. They made more enemies than friends, but without their tenacity and willingness to take grueling punishment, particularly during the lean days of the Thirties, many theatres still available to those who criticize the Shuberts would not now be available.

With the rise of the Shuberts, theatre centralization in New York was further emphasized.

The proof of excellence became the length of the New York run.

Impatient for road returns duplicate companies of New York successes were sent to outlying cities. Soon the "made in New York" stamp became less and less of a recommendation.

The importance of New York as a place of recognition made actors more and more reluctant to go on the road. The dreamed-of opportunity might be lost. Even stars became allergic to travel. Perfection of acting through experience ceased to be the goal. The important objective was New York success.

And then with the quick growth of Hollywood, another goal shone brightly in the western sun, a goal that became still more beckoning with the advent of talking pictures.

Even groups consecrated to the development of art in the theatre were not immune to the Hollywood infection.

One such group of eager, young, consecrated ones so impressed an actor who was prospering in Hollywood, that at considerable cost he bought off his picture contract and joined the group, feeling that their lofty aspirations justified his sacrifice. To his utter and painful disillusionment, one by one of the members of the group took him aside and eagerly asked his advice as to how to get to Hollywood.

This group, in spite of a promising start, was soon abandoned and practically all of its members, from its leading dramatist down, have become old established citizens of Hollywood who do a little theatre puttering on the side when it does not interfere with picture opportunities.

To many, the theatre has become definitely a means and not an end. This is as true of promising dramatists as it is of actors.

The theatre is a proud old lady and knows when she is being used. If she seems less interested in impressing herself than she was of old, it may well be because she, herself, is not at all impressed by the use being made of her.

In a world where visible success has become the high god, it is not strange that the theatre should be infected. The theatre is the world in little. How can the theatre be well when the world is sick?

It is altogether possible that the ills of the world can be identified by diagnosis of the theatre.

I believe that the sole pursuit of success results in half-men, men so completely absorbed by the externals of life that the inner man, the important half of man, is left to atrophy.

Development of half-men in great masses is the calculated aim of Communism. The Marxian dream has degenerated into an intellectual concept of a race wholly devoted to the externals of life, freed of the restraining handicaps of the humanities.

Great obstacles to this realistic advance are the church and the family, so the influences of these decadent forces must be emasculated.

The Communists ascribe the world's ills to the evils of capitalism, knowing that the chief evil of capitalism is the misuse of power.

Capital is not money. Capital is power.

In terms of power Stalin is the greatest capitalist the world has ever known. In the ruthless misuse of power all preceding capitalists shrink into insignificance.

What capitalist in the most selfish days of exploitation could with a negative nod of the head block the world's efforts toward peaceful prevention of a war that threatens annihilation.

Communism is the most effective and corrupting design for the seizure of power that the world has yet encountered.

The great struggle today is between half-men and men who seek to retain some semblance of wholeness, men to whom life without the approval of heart and conscience would be sterile and meaningless—men to whom the inner man is at least as important as the outer man.

Champions of tolerance in other countries, the Communists in their own countries are restrained by no such nonsense as respect for honest opinions. They have quick and fatal answers for such impertinence.

They have used the sword of fear so ruthlessly that they, themselves, are now filled with fear. Their countries are spy-ridden. Born in conspiracy, they smell conspirators wherever they move. Like the old ladies in the empty cathedral, they seek the hidden cause of an unpleasant smell, only to find, on emerging into the fresh air, that it is themselves. The immediate punishment of conspirators is that the stink of their own conspiracy never leaves their nostrils and poisons all decent approach.

The world revolution is deeper than a world being turned upside down. It is the people of the world being turned inside out.

It is the fight between the outer man and the inner man.

Too long the outer man has dominated. Now the outer man and his transgressions have been brought into clear focus by the complete and powerful worshipers of the outer man, the deriders and deniers of the inner man.

No matter what labels are used—Communism, Fascism, Naziism—the content is the same, the half-man, whose god is power, who believes that power, the end, justifies any means, no matter how evil.

No one claims that Democracy has developed a race of

whole men, but Democracy, better than any form of government yet devised, furnishes the climate in which whole men may develop, in which men may fulfill their inner reasons for being.

The theatre is an ideal medium for the development of whole men. Truly creative work is inspirational, the promptings of the inner man. But if the outer man, dazzled by rewards and acclaim, turns away from his inner source, he has lost, or has never found, his only bestowed and inexhaustible point of reference, his contact with the creative force which seeks expression through all of us.

It is difficult for us to learn that of ourselves we are nothing, that no honors or decorations hung on us can make us anything.

Without contact with eternal forces, deeper than conscious mind or unconscious mind, forces that for reasons unknown to us need us as instruments for the furthering of plans beyond our conception, our chief blessing has been wasted, our reason for being unfulfilled. We will have proven ourselves useless instruments.

The quest for the holy grail never ends, but we seek afar when from the beginning it was shining deep in all of us.

It is the light of inspiration. "Let your light so shine" Christ counseled us. It is the light He warned us not to hide under a bushel. It is the Inner Light the mystics found, the Light Eternal. The light of deliverance that a troubled world is now seeking.

May it shine more brightly in the theatre.

# The Fordham Papers

# CHAPTER II

# THE COMMUNITY THEATRE

FOR ONE who has had little faith in academic training for the theatre, I find myself in rather an anomalous position.

I believe there has not only been a great waste of time and money in dramatic schools, but the unkind encouragement of dreams that will rarely be fulfilled.

So, in the past, I have avoided the role of adviser away from the theatre.

My first impluse was to reject Mr. McCleery's invitation to meet with you, particularly when the invitation was for twelve sessions.

I told him, as I now tell you, that I could tell you all I know about the theatre in one session.

But Mr. McCleery assured me that you were very interesting people and could easily fill the time with your own profitable discussions.

It was on that representation that I accepted, so you see the fruitfulness of this session will largely depend upon you.

I will merely conduct a picnic at which you help yourselves to what you have brought.

My first talks will be about the relationship between

the director and the author, and the director and the actor.

If you will indicate to me on what other subjects you would like to base discussions, I will try to open up those fields for you.

I would like there to be some general agreement among you on subjects suggested.

I do not want to take up time in exploring theatre archives. I do not come to you with a vast knowledge of theatre ways of the past, nor do I have much faith in modern experimentation.

Having seen impressionistic and sur-realistic experiments in the heyday of the German theatre, I remain convinced that abstractions in the theatre are distractions.

In the beginning was the word. Anything that detracts from the word is an intrusion, and as such is to be rejected.

We must think of the theatre as a living force and not as a museum in which old bones are articulated.

Of course, in the classic sense there is no time.

Works that still live, will live beyond us.

In the true sense there are no classic revivals, only re-statements of eternal forces that exalt or destroy us.


Before discussing the approaches to theatrical production it might be well to consider the goal we seek. Why are we in the theatre? What do we want of it? Is our impelling urge vanity? Is it hope of personal acclaim? Is it hope of personal gain?

The theatre is a shining lamp for the moth of vanity. The lights of Broadway are symbolic.

Many moths lie dead beneath them. Others have grown

bright wings and flown high. There is higher flying in the theatre than in most pursuits.

Just now, Broadway is an embarkation point for stratospheric flying to Hollywood, and Hollywood an embarkation point to the rest of the world.

High flying was a human dream long before Icarus. Eve doubtless climbed the tree to see and be seen. That she knocked down an apple or two in her descent was her misfortune, and Adam's, and ours.

Climbing mortals ever since have been careless about the fruits they destroyed.

When all of the facts are one day known, we may find that the initial cause of man's tribulations was vanity.

Moses tried to stem the destructive tide with the first commandment, probably the one commandment that every man since has broken.

Vanity is the unashamed badge of selfishness. Had there been no vanity in the world there may have been no wars, no crime, no property, no courts, no harrowing newspapers and surely not the theatre we know.

But for it, I could not have been persuaded to appear before you under the delusion that anything I say might have the slightest effect on your future teaching.

Once we realize that the apple was vanity, we know where the struggle toward wisdom begins. It is the wisdom of Moses, Job, Jesus, Paul, and the mystics before and since them, who knew that God was the only reality and the only Creator.

Since our present aim is to stimulate creative work in ourselves and others, it is important that we fix upon the source of creation.

In Ibsen's "When We Dead Awake" the question is

asked: "What do we learn when we dead awake?" The answer is: "When we dead awake we learn that we have not lived."

What is the barrier to our living? Is it the externalizing of our attention, the turning away from our rich potentials within?

I am sure you do not look to me for spiritual instruction, but I think it important that we agree at the outset that the source of all creative work is within and that no one can impose it from the outside.

In later discussions on the relation of the director to the dramatist, and to the actor, this fundamental will be gone into more fully.

Suffice to say now that I do not believe one person can teach another how to create.

In this series we are not seeking the ways of imitative directing, writing and acting. We are seeking creative ways.

How then, do we begin? I suggest with an appraisal of what we already have in the professional theatre.

What does the commercial theatre offer? The record of the past twenty years is not a proud one.

Playwrights of rich promise in the early twenties have contributed little in the past twenty years.

New playwrights of stature have been too few to fill the vacuum. The development of actors and playwrights is necessarily parallel.

What has happened to the theatre? Where is the stature that it had even in our time? Where is the grandeur, beauty, fury and compassion?

Are we permanently reduced to the competent, unimportant little diversions that are forgotten before we reach the sidewalk? If so, these sessions are not worth our while. The theatre is not worth our while.

How was the theatre lost? Is it lost in us? Have we succumbed to the quick appraisals of a frantic, desperate world? Are we just parts of a great assembly line that leaves us anonymous?

Are we to go on repeating dead words until final words are said over us? Where must we look to find life again?

Many of us know the answer, but do we believe it? Is it the conviction of our hearts, not mere acceptance by our heads?

It is not an easy journey from the head to the heart. This is spiritual schizophrenia, dual being.

Until we reach our own hearts we will not touch the hearts of others. We will not find the right thoughts nor the right words.

Most thoughts and words are skimmed from the common surface. The true riches are unexplored.

They are the waste land never cultivated, the still waters never ruffled by the breath of spirit.

Obviously, in our survey of what we already have, and what we seek, the commercial theatre does not loom as a tower of the future.

But there is a shining tower looming higher now than it ever has, a great potential audience awaiting us.

The theatre's greatest asset is the vast audience that is as yet not touched by it.

Millions of young Americans had to go to war to see their first play.

Many who have returned to their homes in cities, as well as towns, will rarely, or never, see another if they have to wait for the commercial theatre.

In the past fifty years of vast expansion of all activities in America, the theatre is the one institution that has sharply diminished.

When I began, there were regularly five hundred touring companies covering the country.

There were three hundred theatres in the large cities.

There were a hundred permanent stock companies.

Now there are less than one hundred touring companies, less than one hundred theatres in the large cities, and only three permanent stock companies.

In the past twenty years many legitimate theatres have been demolished, or converted, but not one new legitimate theatre has been built.

The theatre, as a national institution, does not exist.

There is little point in exploring the reasons for this disappearance.

Nothing is to be gained by blaming pictures, radio or the greatly increased costs of play productions and operations.

All that we, who are convinced of the importance of the theatre, want to know is—what can we do about it.

Obviously, the grand answer is the professional community theatre—not the little theatre, or the semi-professional theatre, but a thoroughly equipped, amply financed institutional theatre with a long range program of adult plays, unafraid to present the most demanding plays of classical literature, eager to present new plays too hazardous for commercial production.

Each community theatre would have its own school for the development of writers, actors and designers.

Each theatre would send its productions to the smaller communities in its territory.

Eventually, each theatre would have three companies —one playing, one touring, one in preparation. Plays might be presented in changing repertoire, or for fixed runs of limited duration.

Assuming that the theatre solves its financial, personnel and production problems, its chief work will be audience organization.

In this sense the theatre must be taken to the people.

It must be made one of the essentials of full community life.

It passes from the field of diversion, to the field of cultural enrichment, to the field of essential development.

It is something of a shock to learn that in South and Central America one of the chief criticisms of North Americans is that we are people without culture or cultural appreciation.

This is a distrust that extends to Europe and more distant parts of the world.

It speaks well for our neighbors that they consider cultural development essential to fruitful association.

It also explains why, in former peaceful days, they had much closer educational and social ties with European countries than with ours.

If we are to take a commanding position in world respect it is evident that we should have strength that is not wholly economic or utilitarian.

Before the war, as at the present day, in Russia one of the chief cultural voices was the theatre.

One of Lenin's first appointments was Lunicharsky as Minister of Education, entrusted with the developing of the theatre throughout the vast Empire, taking the theatre to parts where it never before had existed.

While, undoubtedly, Lenin thought of the theatre as a political instrument, he simultaneously stamped it as an important medium of education.

The Russian government has never departed from this policy.

In the pressing needs of the past war the theatre and its people were required to maintain uninterrupted pursuit of their own activities. Actors could only function at the front as actors. Their only ammunition was their talent.

Contrast this with the attitude of our government toward the theatre.

In the eyes of Washington the theatre is a frivolous and questionable enterprise, denied release from the federal tax on tickets imposed during the first war, even when similar taxes were removed from firearms, automobiles, jewels, furs and other luxuries.

In the opinion of the Washington tax lords, the theatre is a super-luxury.

During the boondoggling days the government spent twenty-two millions on hastily planned theatre projects, but Mr. Harry Hopkins was careful to point out at the time that it was not a theatre project, but an employment project, so money that might have made a start toward permanent theatre development was spent on a plan that has left no trace of its existence.

This is typical of the American official attitude toward the theatre. This gives government stamp to the impression abroad that we have little cultural appreciation or sense of its importance.

How can there be appreciation of a theatre that does not exist?

How can new talent be developed in a theatre that does not exist?

This is not to be construed a plea for Federal or State subsidy.

I believe the community theatre should belong to the people who support it by their patronage.

It should be their institution and their pride.

It should be a non-profit project, free of Federal, State and local taxes.

It should have the support of all civic organizations, educational institutions, and of labor unions.

It should, in the truest sense, be the people's theatre.

It should not be presented as an objective easily or inexpensively achieved.

It should be presented as a costly enterprise that must be well fortified if it is to survive.

It should ultimately be an institution that grateful adherents will be glad to name in their wills.

Occasionally the Actors' Fund of America receives a gift from an unexpected source, and on investigation finds that the donor felt indebted to the theatre in general for the pleasure it had given him.

I do not believe that a well planned community theatre that has amply provided for its maturing period will be in need of funds.

It will have many problems, but money will not, and should not, be one of them.

The time has come when all people, convinced of the need of the theatre's expansion, should fix upon a goal worthy of their combined thinking and planning.

My chief reason for meeting with you is the hope of awakening in you the determination to be part of this planning.

This is your opportunity to be part of an expanding universe.

The theatre of today is without plan or continued aspiration. Every commercial production is a new enterprise, with no relation to what has gone before, or what is to follow.

Non-commercial productions are equally unrelated to any grand pattern. We know we must envision the dream before the reality appears.

We should not spend this Summer session merely discussing ways of technical improvement. Back of all inquiries the ultimate should be in clear outline and, with Justice Holmes, we must have faith that the picture will fill out as we go along.

What is the function of the theatre?

I believe it is to release the inner potentials of all people concerned—dramatists, actors, audiences, and particularly audiences.

When a thousand people sit before us, appealingly receptive, how are we to enrich them?

Are we to give them stones for bread?

How often in our lives has theatre-going been an experience for which we will be forever grateful?

In my lifetime of theatre-going, here and abroad, the experience has been too rare.

The theatre should be a place of reaffirmation.

In this day of all days we need confirmation of ideals that have been ruthlessly challenged by seekers of power by whatever means.

We need to know that we cannot worship false gods without being destroyed, that there are no devious paths to Utopia, that Utopia is not surprised into surrender and that what we throw away in the attempt is our only passport to Utopia.

That virtue is rewarded and evil punished is not theatrical sentimentality, but unfailing law that the act and the result are one and inseparable.

There is an old adage, "God says, 'Take whatever you like, but you must pay for it.'"

Neither sainthood nor depravity can be obtained without payment.

The person who tries to ride through life without paying ends at no destination. He has actually and spiritually got nowhere. He has died while living. He has not lived.

Many living people can honestly be asked, "Are you sure this trip is necessary?"

The theatre has done, and can do, much toward awakening the awareness of life.

Many people had their first lessons in courtesy in the theatre. Courtesy is more than a grace. It is consideration for others. Out of consideration for others a full rich life can be built.

We are not born with spiritual reservoirs that need no refilling. The theatre in its truest sense is a filling station.

If we will think of that in our choice of plays it will clarify our decisions.

Are we to send people away exalted, compassionate, proud of being human beings, or are we to add to their frustration and cynicism?

Chain reaction did not begin with the atomic bomb. It began with ideas. The theatre is essentially a place of ideas. What chain reactions do we want to set in motion?

When Ibsen wrote "Ghosts" he did not have in mind its possible effect years later on a young Viennese scientist named Ehrlich, yet it was after a performance of "Ghosts" that Erhlich decided to devote the rest of his life to the stamping out of syphilis, so the helpless Oswald was the instrument of delivery from torture and insanity of millions of then unborn victims.

It should also be borne in mind that "Ghosts" was occasionally banned from public performance. In the theatre we can accentuate the positive by accentuating the negative. It is like the two sides of Gertrude's medallion.

If we will continually think of the theatre not as it is, but in terms of its potentials, which are vastly greater than we can know, we will be accelerating a chain reaction that will reach areas of realization far beyond our survey.

If there be one Ehrlich among you who will, one day, demonstrate what is now only our dream, this series will be better justified than by all the instruction we may hope to gather.

In my youth I belonged to a Sunday School class of small, fidgety boys presided over by an elderly lady. One Sunday, to illustrate a point that doubtless had to do with embracing the Lord, she held a watch before the first boy, and said, "Do you want this?" The surprised boy said, "Yes." In turn, she held the watch before each boy and asked the same question. Each boy said, "Yes." At the end, she said, "I have offered this watch to each of you. Each one of you wanted it, but not one of you reached out your hand to take it."

Now, the watch is being offered us. Shall we merely say that we would like it—or shall we reach out our hands and take it?

## QUESTION PERIOD

Were I to start a community theatre I would first seek the co-operation of a non-political civic leader in the forming of a small organizing committee representative of civic, educational and union labor groups.

While seeking no preliminary publicity, the committee should keep local newspaper publishers advised of the contemplated plans and of steps that were being taken.

To one civic group after another the aspirations of the committee should be outlined in open meeting.

It is important from the beginning to make clear that a properly equipped community theatre plant, together with ample reserves for operation, would require between two and three million dollars. It should never be presented as a project easily realized. It should be made clear that from the beginning the theatre is to be professional. It is to be neither amateur nor social. There will be a dramatic school in connection with the theatre. To this, beginners will be admitted without charge. The only requirement for admission will be fitness and character.

Students will be given opportunities in regular performances. On proven ability they will become members of the permanent group.

A list of fifty plays composed of classic and modern plays should be submitted as the source from which productions for the first years will be chosen.

The theatre will give free access to all of its workings to new playwrights of promise, likewise to new scene designers.

Regional plays will be encouraged.

New treatments of old discarded plays will be encouraged.

Regular attendance at this theatre would in time familiarize audiences with all that is best in classic and modern theatre literature.

The chief aim of the theatre would be cultural.

If one community theatre is successfully established it will become a model which other communities will follow and improve upon.

I believe any city with three hundred thousand people to draw upon can maintain a community theatre.

As indicated before, each community theatre could send touring companies to the smaller communities in its area. In this sense it becomes a regional theatre. The extent and activity of this branch is unlimited.

I do not believe in federal government subsidy. This opens supervision that can be disastrous. The Federal Theatre project was abruptly ended by Congressional charges that it had become an instrument for Communist propaganda. Whether the charges were true or not, Congress demonstrated its power to bring to a quick end any government subsidized theatre.

You say that since the Community Theatre is to be the Peoples Theatre it should be subsidized by the government since the government belongs to the people.

My answer is that the government belongs to the people until after election. Then it becomes the instrument of those who have been chosen to administer it. Here personal prejudices are given free sway. The theatre has always been vulnerable to prejudice.

No Community Theatre should be shackled by the fear of angry letters to Congressmen.

Let the community by its patronage determine the worthiness of its own theatre. If patronage fails, the verdict of dismissal will be in the hands of those who supported it and found it unworthy.

It should be made clear from the beginning that no contributor, no matter how generous, has any supervision behind the curtain line.

At no time should the theatre wilfully antagonize any considerable section of the community. It belongs to all of the community.

It should in the best sense be a unifying medium, following the one great reason for its being, revealing to people their own virtues and faults as well as their neighbor's.

You ask if professional actors would be content to leave Broadway for Community Theatre engagements.

My answer is that any actor of aspiration would welcome the opportunity. As things are today it is his only hope of development.

When there are fifty Community Theatres in the country the American theatre will have reached maturity. Its long adolescence has merged into senility. Only the Community Theatre will restore the period of full vigor.

# CHAPTER III

# THE DIRECTOR AND
# CLASSIC PLAYS

SINCE the first step in production is the selection of the play, this session will be devoted to the relation of the producer to the author.

In England, the recognized producer of the play is the director. In America, the producer may be only the promoter, having little to do with the actual production.

For our purpose it will simplify designation if, at all times, we regard the director and the producer as one.

Even in the commercial theatre, a director worth his salt will not accept an assignment under restricted conditions.

He should first approve of the play, the scene designer and the cast, and be the contact with the author, designer and cast who has final authority.

In order to insure these conditions, it is wise for the director, wherever possible, to be his own producer. Division of authority can bring confusion to all concerned.

A play may survive the mistakes of one mind, but its safe passage is endangered by conflicting charts.

The producer is necessarily an autocrat. His authority should not be challenged.

The wise producer will never let his authority obtrude.

He will never give authority as a reason, since that would be acting without reason.

Yet, all concerned with the play should realize that the producer knows exactly what he is seeking and is not on a fishing expedition, wondering what luck may turn up.

This matter of full dependence on the producer will be gone into more fully in another session, which will be devoted to the relation of the director to the actor.

In discussing the relation of the producer to the author, we have two relationships to explore—that with the author who can be present and that with the author who has been called elsewhere.

As all classical drama comes under the second category, we will discuss that first.

Since time is an accepted factor in determining the virtue of literature, we do no injustice to living authors by excluding them, for the present, from the classic category. I am sure they will be glad to delay posthumous glory.

My advice to you in producing classic plays is to place your whole dependence on the author's original work as nearly as you can obtain it.

Do not immerse yourself in the interpretations of others.

Give the dead author credit for having been able to convey clearly just what he meant.

In this adherence to the original, take as a shining example Toscanini, whose eminence has been built on his adherence to the composer's intent which was clearly stated in the original composition.

He has never tried to be the composer's collaborator,

as have other conductors who generously contribute their own special embroidering, which did not occur to the less inventive creator.

Before your time there was a famous clown at the Hippodrome named Marceline.

Marceline's comedy arose out of his eagerness to help others do their special work, and invariably making things worse.

There are many Marcelines in the artistic world—symphony conductors, stage directors, critics and patronizing authorities, with no special qualifications.

As producers, beware of being Marcelines. You will be just as disturbing, not nearly so amusing.

When Toscanini first went to the Metropolitan to conduct a Wagnerian cycle, he astounded the orchestra by occasionally stopping a rehearsal to single out one instrument in the hundred, to say, "That is F, not G."

The indignant instrumentalist would reply, "I've been playing this for thirty years and it always has been F."

"Then your part has been wrong for thirty years. Correct it," ordered Toscanini who, as usual, had no score before him. In this way he pointed out numerous errors. Research proved him right.

A number of able German conductors, Wagnerian authorities, had preceded Toscanini at the Met, but the mistakes were endlessly repeated until his arrival.

Toscanini depended only upon Wagner. I recommend his example to you.

A friend of mine spent many years on cancer research. He once said to me, "The more literature there is on a subject, the less there is known about it. The medical libraries are full of works on cancer."

The theatre libraries are full of works on Shakespeare. I advise you to disregard them.

You will only end up by trying to choose from conflicting conceptions, and whatever you choose will not be your own.

There has been endless discussion as to Hamlet's sanity.

It is quite evident that in several scenes Shakespeare wanted Hamlet to seem insane, but never when Hamlet was alone, or with his friends. Then he was the wise man and mystic.

That would seem quite enough to the producer, yet I have seen one widely hailed Hamlet leap into "To be or not to be" like a mad acrobat, and another enthusiastically acclaimed Hamlet go into apoplectic gyrations with the simple, touching, "Alas, poor Yorick" passage.

This beautiful speech is the one moment of gentleness and peace that Hamlet has in the play. Here, he recalls a happy childhood on whose bright skies no clouds of disintegration or tragedy had yet appeared. How could our frantic English cousin find madness in that.

Victor Hugo's explanation of Hamlet's desire to seem insane is wholly reasonable. In medieval days, superstitious reverence was paid to the insane. The fool was the safest man in court. His insults and breaches of royal respect were found hilarious.

This Hugo concept is borne out by Hamlet impressing his insanity chiefly on Polonius, the court tale-bearer and eavesdropper, and his daughter. What better way could Hamlet have chosen to convince Claudius and Gertrude of his harmlessness?

But Hugo aside, what more do you need than Shakespeare's text. Here Hamlet is to be sane and profound. Here he is to seem insane.

Another great danger in adopting past interpretations is to fall into a pattern which our own experience denies.

As for instance, I give you the endlessly repeated conception of "The Trojan Women."

From beginning to end it is a wailing contest.

We know that there is a point when outrage goes beyond tears and self pity.

Perhaps some day one of you will have the courage to stage "The Trojan Women" with indignation and true, human outrage. If you do, please let me know. I would go a long way to see such an interpretation.

In presenting classics, remember that in the beginning was the word.

In order that the word shall always predominate, have the settings, costumes and lighting as unobtrusive as possible.

The only mission of the physical production is to harmonize with the mood.

Here again non-interference is the most valuable contribution.

The Lord is in His temple. Let all be silent before Him.

When manufacturing jewelers have an especially fine stone, a square cut diamond, or pear shaped emerald, they are careful to so conceal the setting that the stone shines alone in its unobstructed glory.

Be good jewelers when you are setting rare gems of drama.

Someone has said that in poetic writing and reading, the soul speaks.

It is a voice that is easily stifled.

Like contemplation, it is necessarily solitary.

Heighten this detachment. Avoid all distraction. Let the inspired voice be a shining candle in the dark world.

In dealing with living dramatists, different problems arise.

There is only one reason for producing a play—your conviction that the play should be done.

From then on, you become the willing servant of the play.

If you feel that the only reason for producing a play is that it will be a success, you have entered yourself in a guessing contest with the odds against you.

Furthermore, your aims are not toward service, but toward reward.

With success your goal, you introduce an adherence that can easily be bad for the play.

There is a great difference between feeling that a work must be right and that it must succeed.

If success had been the goal, little of the world's art would have been created.

All of life's lessons have been taught long ago. High among the old admonitions is the warning that man cannot serve two masters.

Unfortunately, the world goes on trying the impossible and great and small catastrophes are endlessly repeated.

There is no greater chagrin than the failure of a play that you knew would succeed.

There is no chagrin in the failure of a worthy play that you feel was well done.

Some of my greatest attachments are for plays that failed.

When you do not demand success you are sometimes agreeably surprised.

When I read "What Price Glory," I knew I had to produce it.

It was a war play with no heroics, no romance, no patriotism, no conscious sacrifice.

It violated all of the accepted essentials on which war plays had been founded.

It was bitter, scoffing and profane, but against all of these, it was honest.

We opened in Stamford, and I was prepared for the audience to jeer. Instead of jeers, there were cheers, and the rest you doubtless know.

That play succeeded because we were willing to have it fail.

If we had tried to bend it into a success pattern, it would have failed.

If the author knows it is respect for his work that has moved you to production, you are not likely to find him obdurate in making changes that you think will heighten the impact of his work.

Before you suggest changes, make sure that you and the author are aiming toward the same goal.

Too frequently, suggested changes are really suggestions for a different play than the author has written.

On occasions like this you hear how unreasonable authors can be.

In my experience I have never found authors reluctant to make changes.

The more experienced authors have had newspaper or magazine experience and know that editorial direction can have value.

My chief disagreements, and those not serious, have been about casting.

Under the Dramatists' Guild contract the author must approve the cast, a provision originally intended to protect the author against flagrant miscasting, but now pursued to an unreasonable extent.

It is not my experience that authors have good casting judgment.

To avoid confusion during rehearsal, it is imperative to have all anticipated script changes and the main casting problems agreed upon before going into rehearsal.

Rehearsal time should be a time of no confusion or disagreement.

Everything should aim toward a quiet, easy delivery. Plays have occasionally been born dead because of prenatal hysteria.

Take this out! Throw that away! Put this in! Try this! Get rid of that actor! Just saw an actor who will be just right! Put a chair here—another one over there! Get more flowers! I'm sick of looking at that grandpappy clock! Throw grandpappy out! That's a terrible hat on that girl. Let's see her with her hat off!

Well, is it strange that the child is born dead? It was a wise child that refused to have anything to do with a world of such nonsense.

And then comes the sickening parade of alibis. As you doubtless know, the theatre is the world's greatest incubator of alibis.

The answer to all theatre alibis was given by an illiterate hoofer in the days when legitimate stars occasionally appeared in vaudeville.

It was a Monday afternoon at the Palace. A famous

legitimate male star was making his vaudeville debut. Preceding him on the bill was the hoofer who, for years, had idolized the star. When his act finished, he stood in the wings watching his idol who died slow death, to the consternation of the hoofer.

When the great man came off, the hoofer hurried to him and said, "Don't pay any attention to this audience. They're always tough here on Monday afternoon. By Saturday, you'll be a riot." "Nonsense," glowered the idol, "It's over their heads."

"Yeah," the rebuffed hoofer replied. "Maybe they ducked it."

## QUESTION PERIOD

Perhaps your questions as to what has been significant in the classic theatre in recent years can best be answered by my telling you that for me nothing of deep revelation followed Barrymore's "Hamlet" until the arrival of The Old Vic Company with its overpowering production of "Oedipus" and the even more overpowering portrayal of "Oedipus" by Lawrence Olivier.

Here was theatre of truly classic proportions. There was an over-all pattern, a reciprocal playing that made the group an entity. Moods meshed into each other. When the torch was passed from one player to another the transfer was concealed but the light was constant. There was no sense of abrupt participation or withdrawal. The characters flowed into each other. There were few loose ends dangling from the embroidered whole. It was a group creation. While Oedipus dominated he rarely obtruded. He remained one with the group, finding his impetus from them and returning it to them accelerated and enriched. He made few solo flights. The performance as a whole was what the Baptists hold to be the ideal way to Heaven—total immersion.

Olivier has wisely gone to the only dependable source, the creative stream which lies hidden deep in all of us. He is the free instrument of inspiration unobstructed by calculated externals. He has found visé to the land of revelation, the promised land of creation. He reveals the unexplored areas of self to all of us and exalts us with grateful realization of hitherto unknown possessions.

# CHAPTER IV

# THE DIRECTOR AND MODERN PLAYS

WHAT are the elements in a manuscript that demand production—good writing, good story, good characterization, compelling central idea?

What do you seek—good story, good characterization or central idea?

For at least two centuries the play emphasis has been on story and situation.

It was long the custom of successful French playwrights to determine first the big situation, usually the next to final curtain, and build the play around that.

If the big situation proved sufficiently thrilling success was assured.

Conceive the great moment when the brilliant young lawyer is defending his unknown mother, and "Madam X" is born. The preliminaries and conclusion are comparatively routine.

Audiences patiently sat through dull preliminaries knowing that the great moment was coming to reward them.

American playwrights up to the early 1920's were largely influenced by the French school.

Ibsen had turned the theatre away from romanticism

to realism but, with the exception of Shaw, English and American playwrights were not so much concerned with character analysis and mental conflicts as they were with realistic situations.

One of the highly successful New York producers of the first fifteen years of this century was Al Woods.

His productions of "Within The Law," "The Common Law," "Sign On The Door," "The Green Hat," and a score of others, flooded the country with four, ten or even fifteen duplicate companies. Woods was interested only in the big situations.

On more than one occasion I have seen him in a transport of excitement over a play he had just bought.

With breathless anticipation, he would say; "I don't care what happens to this play. There's one scene I want to see played—just one. Just let me see that scene once, with an audience, and I'm even."

Woods was the best and most successful example of the theatre of his time and I may add, in passing, had an enthusiasm for the theatre that his more academic successors do not approach.

More and more, playwriting has moved away from incident to character and idea.

No more can plays depend on the big act.

Today, the most important act of a play is the act that is being played.

Plays can die in the first fifteen minutes, the last fifteen minutes, or at any time in between.

This is one of the reasons that successful playwriting has grown more difficult.

As soon as I am told that a play is not a play at all, that is one play I want to see.

Even leading critics still believe that in a play something must happen, some problem must be settled in spite of the popular success of such plays as "The Glass Menagerie," "I Remember Mama," "The Magnificent Yankee," "The Late George Apley," and such earlier works as "Victoria Regina," "Disraeli."

It is to be noted that in these cases, the play was really a central character drawing. All was aimed toward a single projection. The incidents were merely vehicles of central character portrayal.

We are living in a "So what" period. This is a deadly challenge to the old sure-fire situations.

What would Camille's dilemma mean to a present day audience.

She has to leave Armand—so what?

With so many problems of wide import confronting people, what interest can there be in purely personal emotional problems having no bearing on such basic problems as how are people to be fed, how are families to be reunited, how are people to find homes, what are people to believe?

This does not mean that any of these problems is a good choice for the playwright.

The point is that the one human element that remains forever interesting is character.

For this reason, I believe that the plays of our time will deal more and more with character and less and less with incident.

When the playwright truly portrays character he reveals to us something of ourselves.

The release is not away from ourselves, but into ourselves, the richest and most unexplored area of our world.

Know thyself is the most neglected of injunctions. Our attention is on externals.

It is the chief mission of the artist to introduce us to ourselves. The artist is ideally man's best friend. He is man's deliverer. He is occupied in God's work—creation and expansion.

He has the understanding heart that Solomon asked the Lord to give him. Solomon did not pray for wisdom, or power, or riches. He asked the Lord for an understanding heart, knowing that this was the one key to true being.

Solomon's prayer should be the prayer of all playwrights, actors and producers.

Granted that a play has qualities that demand production, what must we seek in determining the way of its production.

My first search is for the ignition point.

Just where does the play lose its detachment and become one with the audience.

Some very well written plays have failed because there was no ignition point.

The play and audience remained aloof.

A play requires audience participation.

Sam Harris used to dismiss a play by saying, "There's nothing to root for."

This was what the old playwrights sought to overcome with the big situation.

An ignition point does not mean that suddenly something happens that starts a conflagration.

The ignition may not, at first, be perceptible.

It may glow slowly and the audience be unaware of the forces that are drawing them into the pattern. But the producer should be aware, and from there on he is keeper of the flame.

He must see that it glows warmer and warmer and permit nothing that extinguishes to enter either readings, movements or surroundings.

There should be no arbitrary movement.

There are only two reasons for movement on the stage —emotion or destination.

Any movement that is added for movement's sake, breaks the spell.

It is letting go to take another hold.

In the release, tension has been broken.

The movement in a play should seem so inevitable that there is no realization that the actor has been directed.

In the perfectly directed play, the director's hand never appears.

He is the magician who does not reveal the ways of magic.

He reveals only the result, not the steps of attainment.

The ways of the theatre should be magic ways. The theatre at its best is pure magic.

The theatre is legerdemain and hypnosis.

And always remember that the magic spell is easily broken.

Naturally, the author must contribute to maintaining the spell.

The wrong line, or even word, can break it.

A cherished comedy line may derail a scene quite as effectively as a false melodramatic line.

As in the ideal performance the director is never evident, so should the author never seem to be speaking.

The words are being said for the first time by the characters.

This is the reason that propaganda plays frequently prove pitfalls.

Suddenly the author's voice rings out and the play is shoved aside.

This is the difference between Strindberg and Shaw. In Strindberg only the characters speak. In much of Shaw it is unmistakably Shaw. The mouth is the actor's, but the voice is Shaw's.

Once a play is accepted for production it ceases being the sole expression of the author or producer.

It becomes the new and combined expression of all concerned.

The theatre is essentially a place of collaboration. The more complete the fusion of all expression into one harmonious pattern, the more truly is the work born into a new entity of its own, an entity that may never be achieved again.

Victor Hugo said, "Art is the only true democracy." If the ultimate of democracy is to give full expression to all contributing factors, the theatre is a more complete expression of Hugo's claim than any of the individual arts.

I have always impressed upon casts that there are no unimportant parts in a play.

The actor who has only one line is the pulse beat of the play for that moment.

A lost pulse beat is a moment of death.

In recovering, the heart may lag or beat too feverishly. The rhythm has been lost.

Try always to think of a performance as a living entity.

The common expression that a play died is more than slang dismissal.

It is correct diagnosis, except in those frequent cases where the play never did live. The stillborn are not said to have died, although by some neglect or carelessness they may have been murdered in the process of becoming.

This, too, has happened to plays designed for a better fate.

In thinking of plays as living, we must not confuse living with physical energy.

Life is not to be forced on a play by external applications.

The only source of life is within.

Plays are killed by anxiety, the determination to put them over.

Here they enter the deadly field of salesmanship.

One sure way to rob a play of its appeal is to force it upon the audience. Salesmanship is essentially selfish. It is the frantic seeking for reward, for personal attention and acclaim outside the play.

There are various definitions of ham.

The one true definition of ham is selfishness, disregard of the play for concentration on personal acceptance. Some actors start taking bows with their first speech and continuing taking bows throughout.

There is the slight pause before speaking, which says, "Look at me," needless pauses through the speech, fresh reminders of their shining presence.

I only speak of actors now to remind us that the director, too, frequently disregards the play to let his brilliance step forth and take bows.

The same pitfall yawns for dramatists. They are prone

to do some fine preening outside the framework of their plays.

The dramatist, the actor, the director, should seek only one appellation, the most difficult of all to attain,— "Good and faithful servant."

## QUESTION PERIOD

What has happened to our playwrights? I am sure they are more puzzled about that than you are.

Since the rich writing period of the Twenties ended with the world economic crash, followed by political collapse and war, it is evident that the writer does not find readjustment easy.

The corner soon to be turned seems even farther away from the writer than it was from the optimistic President Hoover.

Attempts to use current problems as play material have not been rewarding. There was no shorthand recording that could keep up with events and constantly changing interpretations.

The one play that made wise and lasting use of world collapse was Thornton Wilder's "Skin Of Our Teeth." As long as mankind is threatened with disintegration this will remain a timeless, wise and affirmative play.

It is significant to note that "Skin Of Our Teeth" is now the most widely hailed play in the rubble of Europe. Any destroyed city is the setting for this play. The inhabitants are the cast.

Like the classic dramatists, Wilder is a poet.

The true dramatic poet is more than a conjurer of symbols and measured phrases.

He is revealer and prophet. He has access to the timeless areas beyond consciousness. To the extent that he reveals to us those hidden regions common to all mankind his revelations remain recognizable and timeless. They are not based on event and are therefore free of calendar limitation.

In Wilder's earlier dramatic works, "Our Town" and his one-act plays, this same exploration of the timeless is the enriching and enduring quality.

Look for future playwrights among the poets.

In addition to Wilder, the present poetic theatre hopes are Eugene O'Neill, Tennessee Williams, William Saroyan, Maxwell Anderson and Lynn Riggs.

Williams' "The Glass Menagerie" is the first major theatre contribution since "Skin Of Our Teeth." This play has the timeless quality of survival. It is a play of human perception, not of event.

Saroyan is imprisoned in his own freedom. When he frees himself from his freedom, he will free us from some of our limitations. He has the rare gift of creating unmistakable character with two or three lines.

I saw a play of his "Hero Of the World" tried out by a small stock company.

The play ran up many alleys seeking treasure, spilling more treasure on the way than it found.

Yet there was one character seen for less than a minute that will remain among my cherished possessions.

A troubled, poor young man is pacing desperately in the hospital corridor outside the delivery room. Suddenly a character not seen, or mentioned before, emerges from the delivery room. He bustles to the young man and says, "Everything's all right. Cost you five dollars if you've got it. If you haven't, here's two cigars—one for you and one for me." Not waiting for a reply he gives the bewildered boy a cigar and hurries away.

There was a tower of gaiety, generosity, compassion, permanently erected in one short speech. That doctor is one of the prizes of my collection.

The first steps toward mature playwrighting in our era were made by Edward Sheldon and Eugene Walter, but it was with the emergence of Eugene O'Neill that American drama took on true stature that won our theatre respectful recognition throughout the world.

For too long a period O'Neill's work had not been seen until the arrival of "The Iceman Cometh."

This play suffered technically from the author's reverence for the indispensable word. Its impact would have been heightened by generous elimination.

Apparently, without the producer's approval the work remained uncut, so the producer became an unwilling accessory to the mistake.

When the author will no longer consider the judgment of his producer, it is a combination of two wrongs that should be lovingly severed.

But more disturbing than the technical faults of the "Iceman" was the author's mistaking as human dream the alcoholic's chronic procrastination of promised deeds. Procrastination is essential to the alcoholic. Only by putting off can he remain an alcoholic.

The destroying dream that he clings to is that whenever he likes he can master alcohol. That this is a deluding dream and can be shattered has been demonstrated many times, most dramatically in these days by the work of Alcoholics Anonymous.

Out of a confused premise grew a play of defeat and pessimism. Pessimism is necessarily a mark of restricted vision, a measuring of the future by the worst of the present, a fallacy so wisely refuted in Wilder's "Skin Of Our Teeth."

In comparison of these opposing appraisals it is Wilder who emerges the wise man.

"Gaze into the abyss" says O'Neill.

"Look up to the hills" says Wilder.

O'Neill remains the master of dramatic speech. His stage is alive and vibrant. His characters need no transfusions from actor or director. The problem is to see that the characters are no less vital than the author has made them.

In my opinion "The Hairy Ape" remains O'Neill's most important work. This is true O'Neill, the inspired dramatic poet. Here are perception, compassion and prophecy.

The world today is full of desperate Yanks, frantically determined to destroy an inhuman scheme that provides no place for them.

The shocking headlines of today were set up by O'Neill thirty years ago.

# CHAPTER V

# THE DIRECTOR AND
# THE ACTOR

GOOD scripts plus good casts make good directors.

The director's most valuable contribution can be in the casting.

An actor who is merely adequate can be the difference between fire and ashes.

There are many competent actors who lack the inflammable quality. The play must carry their weight. With them, the play is truly a vehicle. They have no propelling power of their own. They cannot lift the play off the runway. They are ground mechanics, and as such are useful, but they must be augmented by others who are not earthbound.

This is the reason for the star system.

Stars, properly cast, contribute much more than their names. As an example, see Helen Hayes in "Happy Birthday." Here is a magic demonstration of an actress lifting a play high above the manuscript and the surrounding cast. It is a perfect solo flight.

There are several actresses who could mechanically reproduce all of the actualities of Miss Hayes' performance, but I know of none who could bring such levitation.

Now, obviously, we are entering an area that no director can chart.

We have heard of actors who were made by directors. This is a miracle I have never witnessed.

I have seen disastrous results in the attempt.

A year ago I wrote an article for the New York Times, which expresses my convictions on this point. I will impose them upon you again.

"One of the common mistakes made by those unfamiliar with the theatre is that, by some magic, stage directors can transform people into actors.

"Directors frequently have found nourishment for petted egos in this belief.

"Not infrequently actors, in gratitude, make the same mistake. It would not occur to any of us that we could present another with a talent. Acting talent is as distinctive as writing, painting, engineering, inventing or organizing talent.

"Talent is evidence that the possessor has made way for the creative urge that tries in one form or another to break through all of us. That urge has to knock on a great many inner doors before it gets through. When it is especially fortunate, the medium is called genius. On that basis, every man is a potential genius.

"Like the teacher, or preacher, or philosopher, the highest function of the stage director is to help the seeker open the door to his own riches.

"Neither the director, nor the seeker, is responsible for those riches. From the beginning of time men have only revealed what was always there.

"The old religious hymn dogmatically, but wisely, asserts, 'As it was in the beginning is now and ever shall be.' This is not a denial of growth, but an affirmation of unceasing availability. Eastern and western religious philosophers affirm it as the inner light.

"It is the guiding spirit that the Quakers seek. It is the garden to whose cultivation the irreligious Voltaire believed man should devote himself. Voltaire was speaking of more than cabbages and roses.

"Since creative acting is essentially inspirational, it cannot be acquired by external applications.

"A performance that is hung on an actor by a director is false fruit wired to a tree that has not flowered.

"Too frequently the flowering is prevented by the director. Before the actor has had a chance to bud, the director has burdened him with his own dead fruit.

"There are directors who manipulate set pieces on a miniature stage to work out in advance the movements of a play.

"In the transfer to the stage, the actors remain set pieces, obviously manipulated by wires not at all invisible. These directorial preconceptions have full and deadly play in readings.

"Before an actor has had an opportunity to digest the words, he is subjected to a regurgitating process, which not infrequently sickens him of the whole business.

"Frequently, rehearsals are interrupted by a director giving instructions for which the cast is not yet ready, or to actors who never should have been chosen in the first place.

"If an actor finds it impossible to realize the director's goal, only the director is at fault.

"Either he should not have permitted the actor to continue, or, as a director, he has failed to set in motion the actor's creative potential.

"I have never met the actor who does not want to be good, and that is saying a great deal in these days when pride in work is disappearing.

"The actor may have misconceptions as to approach, or method, but once these are revealed to him he is quick to abandon them.

"Actors welcome help if they feel that the director knows what he wants and is not arbitrarily imposing his will upon them. I have had experience with various stars reputed to be temperamental and unreasonable. I have invariably found stars most anxious for help.

"The director should realize that the sensitive actor, no matter what his previous success, is haunted by the fear of personal failure. The director should free him of this fear.

"Actors quickly sense a lack of confidence on the part of the director. They even imagine it when it isn't there. Paranoia breeds easily on rehearsal stages. Constant nagging helps it along.

"Corrections should never reveal, nor even conceal, contempt.

"Too much direction shuts the actor off from himself. He quite properly complains that he does not feel anything.

"Only a foolish director would disregard this warning and charge it to stupidity or wilfulness.

"If anybody is going to have birth pains at rehearsal, let it be the actors and not the director.

"The director is supposed to be delivering the child.

He cannot even be the implicated parent pacing desperately outside the delivery room.

"Some directors have a very severe accouchement. Their screams can be heard for blocks. No wonder the child is frequently stillborn. It prefers its quiet haven to the Donnybrook outside.

"There is a great deal of 'ham' in directors.

"One famous master of the past spent as much time on his own performance at rehearsal as he did on that of the other actors.

"In essence, a good director knows what he wants, knows how to recognize actors who can give it to him, knows how to arouse their interest in what they are doing, knows how to guide with a friendly hand, convincing the actor that he can succeed.

"In short, the director is a good friend, who understands living characters as well as fictional ones and, above all, likes actors and would rather work with them than any other set of people he has yet encountered.

"Perhaps it all adds up to our old friend, love, of which there is far too little in the hectic commercial theatre."

Following publication of this article I received grateful letters from a number of actors who had obviously suffered under directors who had treated them as pawns.

We must always realize that the chief mission of the theatre is to reveal to ourselves, and to others, the inner riches that are the only surviving essence of all of us.

They are our link with creation.

They have no beginning or end.

They are part of the eternal forces that are always seeking external expression.

In a completely externalized existence these forces are

largely cut off. The world is too much with us. We are too preoccupied with rewards, approval and recognition. We take too little time to seek within ourselves the wisdom and understanding with which we have been entrusted and which we are given freedom to develop or reject.

Again we are reminded of Ibsen's dead who have not lived. They have not fulfilled their reason for being. Life was not given them as an excursion. Man is a two-sided being, the inner man and the outer man.

His mission in life is to find the balance between these two selves. This is rendering unto Caesar the things that are Caesar's, and unto God the things that are God's.

If we will think of the outer man as Caesar, and the inner man as God, we will be able to cast up our own balance and know to what extent we have met this most difficult of challenges.

We need not be told that inspiration has its only source in the inner man.

We know that no man has ever created anything.

Man can only discover what has always been there.

Of what has long been created we still know very little. And yet we are told there are no new frontiers.

Every child that is born is a new frontier.

Every play is a new frontier for the director and actors. We should always be using divining rods to find springs we may never reach.

The director's divining rod must not only seek hidden springs within himself, but hidden springs within the actors. The rewards are sometimes startling and exalting.

When an artist drinks deeply of the inner springs, he is called genius, and the world is refreshed by him long after his passing.

This is present evidence of immortality.

The greatest gift that the director can bring to the actor is faith, faith in the actor's own rich potentials.

## QUESTION PERIOD

As I have told you it has been my experience that stars not only welcome, but are anxious for direction. Like swimmers under water, they need always to know if they are headed in the right direction.

On the first day of rehearsal of "Madame Sand" Mrs. Fiske took me aside and told me that she had worked so long with Mr. Fiske that she hoped I would give her no directions until she felt more at ease in strange surroundings.

I told her that it had not occurred to me that she would need direction. For the first week I devoted myself entirely to others of the cast. Then Mrs. Fiske took me aside and protested that I was helping everyone but her. Of course she needed no help but for her own comfort she needed to know that she needed no help.

It is just as important for actors to know when they are right as when they are wrong.

The aim of all direction should be to give the actor authority.

The actor who plays with authority, authority based on an understanding of the character he is creating, passes beyond the need of detailed guidance: how many steps to take as he speaks—one-two-three-four,—how many beats to count before he speaks,—one-two-three-four,—when to look at a character to whom he is speaking and when to turn away.

The very sense of authority will guide him unfailingly.

And above all he will not need to be told to make himself heard and understood.

In the old days actors spoke of "taking the stage," which meant taking responsibility for what was about to transpire.

Today, too few actors take the stage. They are somewhat indefinite and inaudible parts of what is taking place.

Authority is not to be confused with assurance or assertiveness.

Authority means that the actor's presence is felt by the very rightness of his delineation, by the ease with which he fills out his part of the general pattern, never disappearing and never obtruding.

The actor of authority needs neither stage center nor spotlight.

Wherever he happens to be is stage center.

His spotlight is his own inner illumination.

Too few actors carry their own lighting.

It is the indispensable illumination that makes stars. It is doubtless the reason that they were originally called stars.

Stars are not made by borrowed illumination, no matter how much light a director may think he can deflect from his own rich source.

It is the cold moon that shines by borrowed light from the sun. It is a foolish director who hopes to emulate the sun. The director's only hope is to kindle the actor's own illumination.

By awakening aspiration and giving the actor faith

in his own potentials, much, undoubtedly, has been achieved.

A great deal is said and written about stage technique. I must confess that I do not know what it is.

I would not know by any technique how to create an actor.

Technique is substituting effect for cause.

Technique is dependence upon externals.

Externals develop into tricks.

Tricks are the pitfalls of art.

The director can free the actor from dependence upon tricks by helping him to cultivate authority through clear perception of the character, by faith in his own inner sources.

The director who imposes his own will and conception from the beginning can hope for the emergence of none of these.

In the end he will find himself surrounded by dead moons.

CHAPTER VI

# REHEARSAL APPROACH

IN CHOOSING actors, I depend on the impression I get from talking with them individually, not necessarily about the play, or the part, under consideration.

I seek, first, the quality, rather than the equipment, of the person.

Having had successful results with actors of little experience, I am not deterred by lack of experience if the actor seems to have a quality that is valuable to the part.

Among the then unknown actors who came to me were Clark Gable, Spencer Tracy, Barbara Stanwyck, Roland Young, Louis Wolheim, Guy Kibbee, Brian Donlevy, George Tobias, Hope Williams, Mary Phillips and others.

With the exception of Kibbee they all had little or no experience. Yet each of them had a quality that was at once commanding.

Both Katharine Hepburn and Zita Johann I first saw as unknowns in tryouts, from which they were being dismissed, yet each displayed qualities that could not be mistaken.

The one gift all directors should pray for is quick recognition of the creative quality in others. I believe it is a gift that can be developed if we are sufficiently alert and observing.

In many applicants the artificialities are quickly revealed. These are the first warnings, and for me no others are necessary.

There was once a famous diagnostician, Dr. Frankel, who could frequently identify disease without examination. For him, afflictions had their easily read placards in the face, body or deportment of the victim.

There are character defects that are equally readable to a casting Frankel.

Chief of these is conceit, brassiness, shallowness and an insufferable strain to please.

Beware of disciples of Dale Carnegie.

There is no cause for alarm in timidity, reticence or nervousness. These can be favorable signs.

Others are simplicity, humor, and above all—radiance.

Radiance is the quickest channel of communication. There is no mistaking it when you see it. It cannot be counterfeited. It has carried otherwise limited people to high places in the theatre, as well as in public life. Its absence has left many gifted people among the unrecognized.

Of course, children have radiance, and almost invariably children are good actors.

Few child actors are good in maturity.

Somewhere along the way adjustment to a realistic world has robbed the child of radiance.

A notable exception in the theatre is Helen Hayes, whose glow no facts of life could dim.

Of course, years of rehearsal would never bring an actor

radiance, so if the director is to have it, he must have it from the beginning.

I do not believe in readings for parts.

Some actors are glib first readers. Their ranks have been greatly augmented by radio.

Beware of the good first reading, for frequently it is all you will ever get.

On the other hand, there are gifted people who would never get a part on a first reading.

Indeed, there are some who would be washed out by the Equity five-day rule.

Among actors who have worked with me who showed nothing encouraging in the first days of rehearsal were Laurette Taylor, Lionel Barrymore, Ethel Barrymore and Pauline Lord. As unknowns they would have been in danger of dismissal. They were like distance horses in a race, out-paced for three-quarters of the way, but moving ahead to pass all others at the finish.

Back in the ruck were found the glib first readers. So I warn you against basing your decision on a first reading, good or bad.

In fact, my advice to you is to dispense with test readings altogether.

Listen in conversation for the quality in the voice and in the speech you seek.

Weigh the other attributes of fitness.

It is too early to look for interpretation.

Sometimes the first sound of the voice will tell you what you want to know.

When I was casting "The Petrified Forest" I could think of no one for the part of Duke Mantee. One day I stopped in at the Golden Theatre, where a quick failure was just expiring. Between the ticket door and the stage at the Golden there is a curtain that shuts off the stage. While still behind the curtain I heard a dry, tired voice. Instantly I knew that it was the voice of Duke Mantee.

When I saw the actor I was somewhat taken aback, for he was one I had never much admired. He was an antiquated juvenile who had spent most of his stage life in white pants, swinging a tennis racket.

He seemed as far from the cold-blooded killer as one could get, but the voice persisted, and the voice was Mantee's. So I engaged him, and thus started the catapulting career of Humphrey Bogart.

The first few days of rehearsal are spent in having the actors read the play through, over and over, with few interruptions.

I have the author sit through these readings, looking for script improvements.

This early reading is a basting process.

At its conclusion the cast should be well saturated with the flavor of the play.

I make corrections only in such readings as reveal a misconception of meaning or import.

I do not quibble about emphasis, as long as the meaning is clearly conveyed.

We all have different ways of saying the same thing. And other values being equal I would rather have the actor say it in his own way.

If a director persists in having all lines read as he would read them, he may end by having a group of troubled imitators who have never been permitted to make the play their own.

Obviously, this kind of performance has difficulty in

taking flight. It is the difference between a captive balloon and an airplane.

The true adventure in directing is opening areas of creation that were previously unknown to the actor.

The magic transition in the theatre is from actor to artist. Its revelation is one of the experiences that make the theatre a place of rich reward.

The only area of exploration is within the actor. All directorial supervision should be made favorable to this exploration.

Obviously, the director who keeps pressing his own interpretations shuts the door to the actor's creative channels.

Synthetic actors have been made.

Belasco was credited with this wizardry, but a backward look at his group of wonders reveals that with the exception of Warfield, who was a gifted actor before meeting Belasco, the great man's creations left little imprint on the theatre.

When I first came into the theatre, my direction, or absence of direction, was disconcerting to the actors. They felt lost. Some got the impression that I did not think enough of them to give them my attention. My assurance that they were progressing was sometimes not enough.

Unaccustomed to finding their own way, they mistrusted their own sense of direction. The first audience reaction was a great surprise to many of them.

For some time the myth persisted that I did not really direct at all, a myth for which I was responsible, since that was the effect I sought.

Dorothy Parker when asked about my method of direction—called it absent treatment.

In the early days I arranged a production of Clare Kummer's "A Successful Calamity" with William Gillette.

Gillette had always directed his own plays, and was something of a martinet. He was all that is conveyed by that frightening word—meticulous. He was really meticulous down to the last inflection and movement. He followed a very effective system for him. His device was to have everyone else over-act, while he under-acted. This left him in easy command of all situations. He could still confusion with the lift of a finger or by calmly lighting a pipe. It gave all of his work a heightened authority.

You see the same technique now successfully used by movie actors of the Alan Ladd type.

Of course, my method of direction seemed aimless to Gillette. It became quite evident that he felt nothing was being accomplished when, after two weeks, he said to me, "I hope, Hopkins, we'll not have to open if we're not ready." "Of course, not," I replied, "but I think we'll be ready. It's coming along fine." Then he knew he was in bad company, so said no more.

When Gillette and I made our arrangements he told me he wanted the right to buy a third interest in the play. I, of course, agreed. There was no contract. In those days, most contracts were verbal.

Gillette, as you know, was a New Englander. On the day we were to open in Atlantic City, he said to me, walking up the boardwalk to the theatre, "Now, Hopkins, you understand if this play is a failure, I want to pay my twenty-five percent of the loss." He was saving eight and a third percent out of the wreck.

"Oh, don't trouble about that," I said. "I think we'll be all right."

A bewildered Gillette saw the play a success. After three weeks in New York, the production cost was recovered. On the fourth week I sent Gillette a check for a third of the week's profits.

I was curious to see what he would say. I am still curious . . . He said nothing.

If, from any of this, you gather that Gillette was a timid man, afraid of failure or loss, I will have misled you. He was one of the giants of his day, an artist of true distinction, gifted, humorous and wholly devoted to the theatre. In private life he was a recluse, never seen in public places, refusing all interviews and above currying approval or attention. But he had gone all his life believing that supporting actors would not register if they followed his own simple, honest method.

In "Calamity" he was surrounded, for the first time, by a cast that played just as simply and honestly as he, and to his great surprise, helped him to one of his greatest successes.

Upon hearing recently, at the Harvard Theatre Collection, a recording of a scene from "Othello" made by Edwin Booth in the early Nineties, I became convinced that Booth had been the great influence on Gillette's career.

In this recording Booth reveals a simple method, wholly free of Shakespearean exaggerations, an earnestness so honest and compelling that one understands at once his high acclaim in both America and England.

It was said of Booth that no one could do a travesty of him. When you hear this record you will understand why.

He had none of the eccentricities or exaggerations that are essential pegs for travesty.

To Gillette I shall always be indebted for one much needed lesson—a proper appraisal of dramatic criticism.

I had heard that few of the stars of that day ever read reviews. I was later to learn that this was true. To the aristocracy of the theatre it was a mark of deference, which they did not feel.

I was young, easily flattered, and an open target for good notices. The New York notices for Gillette and the play were so unanimously enthusiastic that I was struck with a great idea. I would not quote the critics. I would thank them.

So the Sunday papers carried a dignified and grateful announcement which only said, "To The Dramatic Critics—We thank you."

Now that might not have been so bad, but under the "We thank you" I added the names William Gillette, Clare Kummer, Arthur Hopkins. Well!!!!

I stopped in Gillette's dressing room the next evening, enormously pleased with myself, and there met a block of New England granite.

In a cold, bitterly courteous voice, Gillette told me that he had never thanked a dramatic critic in his life, in fact, had never spoken to one, that he did not propose at his time of life to express a veneration that he had never felt, nor did he relish having me do it for him, so if I valued his association I would desist.

Now this from Gillette was doubly strange, since for years he had always had the most laudatory approval of critics.

Later, when I encountered this same resistance in association with other stars of that period, I began to understand.

To them critics were outsiders, authorities who had served no apprenticeship in a field that is not easily appraised, men who could only enter the front door. They had no vise for the stage door, the only sesame to a position of informed theatre appraisal.

If the Gillette incidents seem a digression, I am sure you will realize their pertinence.

To resume rehearsals. We have passed the early days of reading and now the actors are on their feet. I have previously settled in my mind about where the areas of action are to be. Now, without stopping for reading values, the actors are shown the general movement and positions of the first act. This usually takes about an hour. I keep the actors on this act for about two days, going over and over it, with few stops.

This is another basting period, another period of complete familiarization and immersion.

Frequently, at the end of this period, some of the actors need little or no instruction. When instruction is necessary, I take the actor aside and show him where I feel he is going wrong.

When I feel an actor is on the right track I tell him so in the presence of the others. Usually, an actor will hold on to what has been openly approved.

As a rule, I do not proceed to the second act until I feel that both the script and performance of the first act approximate their final form.

The following acts are each developed in the same way. Unless we have run into script or casting trouble, the play is generally set for a run-through in ten days.

This leaves two weeks for the polishing and liberating processes.

Script changes, except for minor ones, are not discussed or made at rehearsal.

These are gone over with the dramatist. The remedy is agreed upon.

When the new material is acceptable to both of us, it is given to the cast.

As you see, every effort is made from the beginning to avoid uncertainty and confusion.

I believe that inner peace and quiet is essential climate for creative functioning.

I do not believe in long, wearisome rehearsals, rarely holding the cast for more than six hours a day.

Above all, I avoid going over and over individual scenes until they have lost their original flavor and impact.

Actors can get sick of a scene, or of a play. When the first sign of that nausea appears, it is time for everyone to take a rest.

When rehearsing becomes an ordeal very little good will come of it.

Spontaneity is a precious metal that must not be refined to extinction.

As I have pointed out to you before, only essential movement is used, care being taken that people are not obviously jockeyed into position.

Actors must play to each other—not to the audience. This frequently places an actor with his back partly, or wholly, to the audience. This helps free the stage from its flat two dimensional restriction.

Treat the stage as a circle, not as a parallelogram.

A well-staged play will look as convincing from the back-stage wall as from the orchestra pit.

The purpose of the circular concept is to make the play a self-contained entity, not living because of, or for, an audience.

The play is not to be taken to the audience.

The audience is to be drawn into the play.

This is the meaning of transport.

No audience is carried away by a performance that is put in its lap.

Never tell an actor that he is responsible for a desired effect.

The actor has only one responsibility—to make the character honestly live.

He cannot serve two masters, the audience and the part. His only master is the part.

Never upbraid an actor for not getting a laugh, unless he has lost the laugh by trying for it.

In that case, upbraid him, whether he gets the laugh or not.

Actors are not peddlers.

The good director will never degrade them to pandering.

This truth was stated centuries ago by Confucius, who was not speaking of actors, but was contrasting the superior man to the inferior man.

He wrote, "The superior man knows what is right. The inferior man knows what will sell."

Encourage your actors to be superior men.

## *QUESTION PERIOD*

The director is prone to forget that material familiar to him is, at the beginning, unfamiliar to the cast. His early rehearsals should be wholly devoted to overcoming that difference.

He should clearly outline to the cast the pattern of the play as he envisions it, and the relation of the parts to the whole.

It is not only important for the cast to know what the play is about, but how the director plans to interpret it. This not only simplifies the actor's individual approach, but gives him a sense of responsibility for the group effect.

Not only must he contribute to the whole, but he must do nothing that detracts from the whole.

The mission of the director is to combine individual talents into a group talent.

Once this aim is clearly understood it is interesting to note with what ease, and apparent relief, actors of selfish repute depart from their old troublesome ways.

The temperamental one learns that this protection of the whole is also protection for him, that while he may do nothing to detract from others no one else may detract from him.

Fear of detraction by others haunts the sensitive actor, and understandably so, for he has suffered sore afflictions from fly-catchers in the past.

The director must understand that the only cause for temperamental outbursts in the theatre is fear.

The angry star is a frightened star.

Once the star realizes that he has the director's protection, he becomes a willing collaborator.

I have never known a star to object to another actor because he was too good. I have never seen jealousy the cause of dissension.

This protecting attitude of the director is just as important to the small part actor as to the star. The more he feels he belongs, and is important, the more certainty he will contribute.

In the early rehearsals of "Macbeth" I was startled by an unexpected outbreak from the Lady of the play. She began loudly berating a trembling beginner, who was playing a messenger.

I stopped rehearsal to remind the Lady that the messenger, and all others of the cast, were quite as important to the play as she and just as much entitled to respect, and if she did not realize that obvious fact she was in the wrong theatre. She decided she was in the right theatre—and that was the end of outbursts that might have made life miserable for everyone throughout rehearsals.

When joy goes out of the theatre it is no place to be.

The rehearsal period should be the richest experience in the theatre.

It is the one reward that actors and director can treasure long after the fate of the play has been decided, no matter what the decision be.

The actor who feels that life begins with the first performance has missed the best part of theatre living. He has spent the honeymoon worrying about the hotel bill.

The temptation to tell others exactly how to do things is a human failing from which directors are not free.

But the director, because he is in a unique position to impose this failing on others, must realize that it is a failing and free himself from its evils.

He must give the actor opportunity to develop his own resources. It is then the duty of the director to guide and make the best possible use of what the actor reveals.

In the end, it should be the actor's creation and not the director's. Only thus will the creation be firmly imbedded and authoritative.

What the director hangs on the actor never becomes part of him.

The only firm foundation for a creative structure is deep within the actor.

Creative acting cannot be prefabricated by the director.

Long discussions of character implications should be avoided.

Contrary to Stanislavski, I think fruitless and frequently absurd the attempt of the actor to reconstruct the character's life prior to his appearance in the play or what the character is busying himself with in the periods when he is off the stage. Such pursuits can easily fabricate a character which was at no time in the author's mind. The actor thus becomes an uninvited collaborator of the author.

The only collaboration the author requires is complete understanding of the character's motivation as the author has revealed it.

If the author feels that events before or outside the play are needed to explain the character's reactions to events within the play it is for him to provide the explanation.

You ask the difference between the interpretive actor and the creative actor.

It is the difference between the actor and the artist, between imitation of life and the creation of life.

The same distinction is to be found in all of the arts.

There are many gifted imitators, but few creators of original work.

Acting at its best is not imitation of life. It is recreation of life.

# CHAPTER VII

# REVELATIONS IN ACTING

IN MY early theatre days I wrote, produced and booked vaudeville acts. There was great art in the vaudeville of that day. To that experience I owe much.

Vaudeville audiences were alert and knowing. They were quick to detect the phony, and quicker still to reject the dull.

It was the most thoroughly trained audience that the American theatre has known. They rarely missed their weekly lesson. Some legitimate actors of reputation failed miserably in this alert company.

Yet, it was in this challenging atmosphere that artists wholly free of audience consciousness reigned supreme. They were only concerned with accurate portrayal. The audiences could take it, or leave it.

They gave the sense of things truly happening, truly being created, that was rarely to be found in the legitimate theatre. They had a magnificent indifference to effect. No audience approval or indifference could deflect their aim.

They neither expanded with approval, nor shriveled with indifference. They seemed to say, "This is the way it is. The rest is up to you."

It is remarkable that this rich integrity should have

flourished in a field where so much was brash and frankly objective.

Yet, these carriers of the banner of integrity were those dearest to the hearts of armies of vaudeville adherents who had seen them over and over, and could never see them too often.

High in the list were McIntyre and Heath, Howard and North, Clayton White and Marie Stuart, Ryan and Richfield, Tom Nawn, Victor Moore and Emma Littlefield, Ed. Blondell, Cressy and Dane, Roger Imhoff, Charlie Case and others.

These were the aristocracy of vaudeville. Their position was unquestioned. Their bookings were never in doubt. They were a clannish lot, who had little interest in the world outside of vaudeville. The one characteristic of all was that they were quiet people. A temperamental, or conceited, or selfish intruder soon found himself alone. They had no time for such stupidity, and had scathing terms of dismissal.

If they found a theatre manager rude, or objectionable, his chances of booking them again were remote. They never worried about results.

When Harry Lauder arrived in New York for his first appearance, a timorous friend said to the stocky Scot, "Harry, I'm afraid they'll no understand you here." His reply was, "The boat sails Saturday."

I saw his opening matinee at the New York Theatre. He was supposed to do about twenty minutes. He had difficulty in getting off the stage after an hour and a half. So the boat sailed Saturday without him.

The most perfectly co-ordinated acting team I have ever seen was McIntyre and Heath. For over fifty years

they played their black face sketches, "The Georgia
Minstrels," "The Man From Wyoming," "On Guard,"
and other classics of their own creation.

None of these sketches had been written.

They were improvised in the way of old afterpieces,
the comedia del arts of vaudeville and burlesque.

The young McIntyre would suggest, "Now you say this
—and I'll say that," and Heath might say, "Or, maybe
it'll be better this way," and so through years of saying
this and saying that, they had built up gems of character
study, which had become firmly fixed long before the
time I was to see them.

Despite thousands of repetitions, the last performance
had that ultimate of stage magic, the sense that everything was being said and heard by them for the first
time.

In those days of two-men teams, there was usually a
straight man and a comedian, the comedian having all
the answers and the laughs.

With McIntyre and Heath it was impossible to desig-
nate the straight man. Both were comedians, and by their
quality of earnestness both were straight men.

Amos and Andy were a faint radio copy, Amos being
something like the timid McIntyre. It was with the introduction of Kingfish that the Heath replica appeared.

In the portrayal of the stranded, foot-sore, hungry
Georgia Minstrels, Heath painted maddening pictures of
a magic land to which he was leading his starved com-
panion, a land where hams grew on trees, and where
flowed the peaceful beer river. Here were perfect pictures
of the defeated and the undaunted.

Here, in miniature, was a magnificent portrayal of the

age-old vicissitudes and hopes of man in the muck seeking the high ground. Here was mythology and man.

Each sketch was a broad canvas in a simple frame.

The thoughts and reactions were so much a part of the two magicians who revealed them that I doubt if the words in other mouths could have much significance.

Again it is interesting to note that these words were never written.

For over fifty years these men held their twice daily ceremonials.

Old and rich, it never occurred to them to stop, this, in spite of the fact that in their later years, they never spoke to each other except on the stage.

Some unknown misunderstanding had erected a barrier of bitterness between them, but never a sign of this bitterness appeared in their performance. Here again, they were one. Perhaps that was why they would not give up playing.

When Tom Heath was dying he asked them to send for Jim. Jim came. They were left alone together, these two young dreamers from Texas, who carried their dreams through honky-tonks and beer halls to the highest peak of stage artistry.

Now they are both gone, perhaps still searching for that magic land where the ham tree grows.

I stop to honor them, because if any of you get anything from me, it is, in part, what I bring to you from them.

Howard and North did a series of sketches called "Back To Wellington," Howard portraying a country boy who had gone to the city and acquired its noise, brassiness and contempt for simple ways.

North, remaining on the farm, had found the contentment and philosophy of the undemanding life. You can see again that this was an epic canvas in miniature. The emptiness of selfish aspirations and the fullness of unselfish service and devotion are inherently classic materials for contemplation.

With the passing of vaudeville Howard and North disappeared, North, true to form, to a cracker barrel in a small Jersey town. He was one of the great comedians, an unfaltering artist.

When I was casting "The Old Soak," my one wish was to have North play the lead, Don Marquis' small town philosophical ne'er-do-well, Clem Hawley, but it was wishing for the moon. North would not even come to town to talk about the play. There was nothing in the city, or the theatre, that he wanted.

So you see, he knew all those years what he had been playing. Some of him, too, I bring to you.

To my mind, the truest artist among the monologists was Charlie Case.

As you may know, monologists were usually breezy Bob Hope fellows with stories they had collected from many sources. They were frankly objective, and frequently objectionable.

Case was none of that.

He was a timorous, rather frail mulatto, who disguised himself by blacking up. He wore an old, tight evening suit and whitecotton gloves. He disposed of his nervous hands and all gestures by constantly winding and unwinding a piece of string on his index fingers.

He spoke with no dialect, in a rather thin, pathetic voice. He wrote his own material, and all of his stories were about his family—his father, mother, sister and brother—and their dilemmas. The stories were funny and touching. This famous one I am sure some of you have heard:

"You know, it's a funny thing, Mother can always tell when Father's been drinking. My brother and I can't tell. We hear a noise on the porch. Mother goes to the door, opens it, turns to us and says, 'Boys, your father's drunk again.' We go and look. We can't tell. We think he's dead."

There were countless stories with an occasional song of his own composition, sung without accompaniment and with only a faint trace of voice. These songs were travesties of the sentimental ballad, and were merciless.

One was called, "That Little Old Red Merino Dress My Sister Wore." I am sure the title reveals to you its comic possibilities.

This amazing man never recovered from stage fright. Each appearance was a harrowing ordeal, but he went on year after year lightening hearts of others while his own remained perpetually troubled.

He finally destroyed himself.

Some of that rare artist I also bring to you.

Now Charlie Case actually did nothing in the usual sense of doing. He would have been the despair of an elocution teacher, or of a stage director. He stood still in one spot, with no movement, but the industrious winding and unwinding of the string. His speech was without emphasis. He used none of the conventional externals.

He was the perfect example of the artist drawing the audience to him while not seeming to realize its presence, and he was one of the great successes of his time.

I have given you but a few instances of this valiant band. The mark of all of them was integrity and simplicity. These people came from mines and farms and shops. Few of them had early education, none of them had training.

They found their way into tent shows, rep companies, minstrel shows, show boats, dime museums, mining camp saloons, seeing gold everywhere but never having any of their own.

Now, of course, none of them had ever encountered stage direction as we know it.

And this is the point at which we must stop and think.

How much was the absence of direction responsible for the perfection they had attained?

Would they have gone as far if someone else had imposed his conceptions upon them?

What would they have lost in the process?

In my opinion they would have been in danger of denial to what made them—free access to their own resources.

These people had really cultivated their own gardens. The fruit was always fresh, because they, themselves, were the trees that bore it.

There was never the staleness that is the blight of legitimate plays after comparatively slight repetition.

The fruit that a director hangs on an actor's tree easily goes stale. It has the continued nourishment of neither the director's tree nor the actor's tree.

Plainly, the director's only lasting contribution is to make way for the actor to cultivate his own garden.

A director of perception recognizes blight when he sees it, and reveals it to the actor, but if he wants a healthy crop he does not dispossess the actor and take over the garden.

Then it becomes nobody's garden and will soon lie barren.

How often have you seen a director push an actor aside and play the scene himself?

Mark him as a garden vandal, a planter of mock fruit.

The director must pray for patience, perception and faith, faith that creation seeks expression through all of us and belief that none of us was given sole access to the eternal springs.

Above all, the director should never be a boss.

Bosses may have their place in menial work, though I doubt even that, but there is no room for a boss in a theatre.

May all casts be delivered from the lint-picking director, the little man with a microscope.

From the director who inflicts his barbed jokes on defenseless people.

From the director who suffers the tortures of the delivery room.

From the hysterical director, a fugitive from the home for wayward girls.

From the director who keeps actors waiting while he is prostrate with exhaustion.

From the director who keeps actors sitting around while he tries to make up that rumpled bed—his mind.

From the director who stages a big scene which he has planned for his own stellar appearance.

One of those planned scenes was once rudely derailed by the gods of derision.

There was a stage battle-ship afloat on a cupful of stage

sea. There was a moment when sailors had to dive into the shallow water. The actors managed as best they could to come up wet. The director was scornful. "It's nothing like it, nothing. Wait, I'll show you."

To everyone's amazement, he began to undress, and by the strangest coincidence he had a bathing suit on under his clothes. He mounted the ship ladder, poised beautifully for a moment on the rail, and gave his rather awkward conception of a swan dive.

Then the gods stepped in. He came up sputtering through a bloody nose.

Now what kind of a mind is it that would start its day by putting on a bathing suit to go to rehearsal.

I am happy to report that Hollywood captured this diving beauty and the theatre has seen nothing of his curves for years.

One of the classic sufferers was an actor-director who, on one occasion, at the conclusion of a bad dress rehearsal, knelt on the stage, raised his arms to Heaven and cried out: "Lord, you are my witness I've done all I can with these people. They are out of my hands now. I leave them to You." A transference that was made too late.

Another famous director had a stock of dollar watches. When his pre-arranged scene came, he climaxed it by shattering his priceless dollar watch on the stage.

But one day, through some underling's blunder in making the switch, he really smashed his priceless watch. When he saw what he had done his rage was no longer thespian. Then he really depicted rage. The underlings were hours trying to put Humpty-Dumpty together again.

Contrast these absurdities with my vaudeville friends

and you will understand why I took a different path to direction.

While there are fewer absurdities on the stage today, there are still the inflictions of ego and fear, there is still the frantic urge of salesmanship.

There is still the taint of mendicancy.

There is still the pathetically soliciting appeal of prostitution.

I was once asked by the Encyclopedia Britannica for a definition of Stage Direction.

I could think of nothing that would at once make clear to the layman what Stage Direction is, and what I think it should be. I now have a similar request from Collier's Encyclopedia, and am no less puzzled.

The stage director occupies a position unlike that of any other contributor to the arts. As has been demonstrated for centuries, he can be done without altogether.

As has been often demonstrated, the director can do more harm than good.

If the director's work is perfect, audiences will not be conscious of it. That is the proof of perfection.

The ideal director is a body that radiates light, but throws no shadow.

The ideal director is a seismograph that records hidden motion, motion within the actor.

The ideal director is a divining rod who locates untapped springs in others and brings their living water to the surface.

The ideal director reveals the goal which all are to seek.

The ideal director envisions the whole pattern, and knows when it is being distorted or unfilled.

The ideal director is the flavor in which all are immersed.

The ideal director is the presence that remains after the person has gone.

The ideal director is a fore-runner of creation.

The ideal director is an escort and guide of creation.

The ideal director does not exist. He is in the long process of becoming.

The ideal director's cry is, "Make Way For The Lord Creator." He makes way for the Creator in others by making way for the Creator in himself.

Make way for the Lord Creator!

## QUESTION PERIOD

No, it must never be left to the actor to do as he pleases.

Freedom must not be mistaken for absence of correction.

The director is solely responsible for the final result.

The director must, at all times, have the whole pattern in clear view to himself and the cast.

The balance between restriction and license, or unfulfillment, must be maintained.

It is much the same as the symphony director's problem, except that a composer's score is more exact than a dramatist's can possibly be.

Again I remind you that the director's function is to blend all of the elements of a production into a single entity that takes on a life wholly its own.

When the director has attained an over-all effect that

cannot be appraised in terms of separate contribution, he has achieved his goal.

The theatre at its best is magic.

The means, or method, of attainment should not be discernible.

When the mechanics of a play are evident, the play has not been well done.

This applies particularly to movement.

Movement should have an inevitability that conceals direction.

It is not my plan to advise you in imitative ways of direction. It is my hope to instill in you an attitude toward direction that will free you from its temptations and evils.

Once your attitude is firmly fixed, details of direction will find consistent solution.

The director's work should always bear a recognizable signature.

Let your signature be integrity, the integrity of all concerned.

Yes, the vaudeville of old has disappeared. Its disappearance was chiefly due to the failure of new talent to develop. Programs became more and more objective.

Vulgarities that long had been rigidly banned became more and more common.

The artist was replaced by the eager salesman.

The final and crowning imposition was the master of ceremonies.

With this irrepressible interrupter, augmented by jazz bands, vaudeville took on a garish night club aspect.

With change in pattern the audiences changed. The family aspect disappeared.

B. F. Keith, father of vaudeville, always thought of it,

and planned it, as family entertainment. In this way future audiences were recruited among the young. When the family and the young disappeared from vaudeville audiences, the end was in sight. Instead, the young were attracted to the new contender—silent pictures.

The disappearance of vaudeville was a great loss to the legitimate theatre.

It had been the training ground of such stars as Montgomery and Stone, Elsie Janis, Marilyn Miller, Nora Bayes, Florence Moore, W. C. Fields, Will Rogers, Walter Huston, Al Jolson, Eddie Cantor, Bobby Clark, Frank Tinney, Fannie Brice, Bert Lahr, and other valiants.

The vulgarization that helped destroy vaudeville is now too frequently evident in the legitimate theatre, an omen that should not be disregarded.

# CHAPTER VIII

# UNNOTED PRECEPTS

In Thornton Wilder's "The Skin Of Our Teeth," the fortune-teller says, "It is easy to read the future, but who can read the past?"

All wise instruction for man's fruitful and peaceful living was set down long ago, but who of us accepts them? Long, dreary months are spent over the haggling peace table. Mistrusting statesmen try to work out elaborate plans which will guard the future against destruction, but the right words do not come. And there they are for all men to read in The Sermon On The Mount, but who can read them?

Hitler employed astrologers to read the future, and yet, in the past his fate had been clearly set down. The Old Testament prophets described him and his collapse, even to his final evaporation. Consider!

Though the wicked man's head reach into the clouds, he shall perish forever like his own dung.—

He shall neither have son nor daughter among his people, nor any remaining in his dwelling.—

They that come after him shall be astonished at his day, as they that went before were affrighted.—

For his heart has trusted in wickedness.—

Therefore, evil has come upon him and he is not able to put it off.—

The eye which saw him shall see him no more, neither shall his place any more behold him.—

They that have seen him shall say, "Where is he?"—

He shall fly away as a dream and shall not be found, yea he shall be chased away as a vision in the night.—

God shall destroy him forever, root him out of the land of the living.—

Let now his astrologers, his star-gazers, his monthly prognosticators stand up and save him from the thing that has come upon him.—

Well, there it all was for Hitler to have read. No biographer can draw a truer picture of him, or his fate, than was set down by the prophets thousands of years ago. If the hysterical one had been able to read the meaning of "War And Peace," Tolstoy would have saved Hitler a trip to Russia.

Men write learned and troubled discourses trying to find answers that are simply stated in a single sentence uttered by Jesus, or Lao Tse, or Plato, or Lincoln.

And so it is in the theatre.

All that ever need be said about the externals of acting was said by Shakespeare in Hamlet's speech to the players. And yet how many Hamlets who have read that speech trippingly, have ever read its meaning?

This is the one speech in "Hamlet" where Shakespeare departs from the play long enough to voice the bitterness of the author whose words had been too often outraged. This is definitely the author, and not Hamlet, speaking.

This speech could not have been written by a man who

had not been deeply and painfully immersed in the out-
rages of the theatre. This one speech, to my mind, does
much to dispose of the Bacon claimants. This was not
written by a closet scientist who had no active traffic with
the theatre and its tribulations.

The speech is rather pathetic, too, for Shakespeare was
willing to settle for so little.

His requests were confined to externals. There were
few dos, chiefly don'ts. He did not ask for perception, or
conception, or even understanding.

He merely asked them not to mouth the words, not
to saw the air too much with their hands, not to tear passion to tatters, not to play to the groundlings. Only to do
what was fitting in conveying the modesty of nature, not
to make the judicious grieve, "the censure of which one
must, in your allowance, o'erweigh a whole theatre of
others."

It is interesting to note that the only criticism he re-
sents is praise for bad work. Here, again, he is the true
man of the theatre, for there is no greater resentment
among theatre people than praise for one who has not
earned it.

There were obviously Marcelines and busy salesmen
in Shakespeare's day, for he deplores those who speak
more than is set down for them, or who "themselves laugh
to set on some quantity of barren spectators to laugh too,
though, in the meantime, some necessary question of the
play be then to be considered."

There you have Elizabethan peddling and scene steal-
ing.

Now all of these simple and undemanding words were

set down centuries ago by the one god of our theatre, yet actors of our day cannot read the past. They daily violate all of these easily fulfilled precepts.

My first close observation of the legitimate theatre, other than as a spectator, convinced me that it lacked both the honesty and the creative art that were to be found in vaudeville. Although there was a wealth of acting talent in that day, it seemed to lack cohesion and clear pattern.

Too frequently, it was individual, rather than group impact. In other words, there seemed a lack of general direction.

There was a great deal of meticulous direction, which had been brought to realistic perfection by Belasco.

There was the more imaginative direction of Winthrop Ames who, to my mind, was the most progressive director of his time.

There was an over-all competence in the Frohman productions, and in the productions of Mrs. Fiske, yet none seemed to be free of audience consciousness.

The stage had not liberated itself in the sense that the vaudeville explorers had liberated themselves. It had not found the same high ground, nor did it breathe the same creative air. Legitimate performance was a balloon that frequently soared high, but remained a captive balloon.

Occasionally an actor broke the accepted mold, and at once something extraordinary happened.

My first revelation was through the then inconspicuous Lionel Barrymore, who was playing a small part with John Drew in "The Mummy And The Humming Bird."

Playing an Italian organ-grinder, he had but one brief scene, yet for that magic interlude the stage was transformed, liberated. It became something beyond competence, beyond pretense, beyond approval. It was—that's all. It just was, and there was no other.

It happened again when Laurette Taylor was playing a secondary part in "Alias Jimmy Valentine." There was no analyzing the effect, or the way of its attainment, but obviously if hers was acting, then no one around her was acting.

Miss Taylor had many magic moments after that, but to the end her ways of attainment remained a mystery. She drove to desperation other stars who tried to discover her secret. She did nothing anyone else could make use of. Her gestures were scarcely gestures at all. Her readings were not seemingly aimed for effect. Yet, the effect kept mounting, never wavering, never over-reaching, but always mounting.

Of course, she could not be appraised in terms of acting, for she had progressed from actress to artist.

In art, the technique disappears.

She became a presence as Duse was a presence, as Booth was doubtless a presence.

Presence cannot be imitated.

Her supreme gift was radiance. Even when that unforgettable face was old and ravaged, it could suddenly be illumined by beauty that is not of this earth. She was a star of celestial illumination.

Again the miracle happened when an unknown actress appeared in "The Talker" with Tully Marshall and Lillian Albertson. The unknown was Pauline Lord.

When I was looking for an actress to play the lead in a road company of "On Trial" I knew she was the one. With difficulty I located this shy and self-effacing girl. Apparently, she was little interested in playing.

When she opened, there again was the miracle, acting that was not acting at all, piognancy that came from deep and troubled wells. I told her I would find a play for her.

We were three years waiting for the particular play, but it came when George Jean Nathan sent me Eugene O'Neill's "Anna Christie."

In the meantime, she had made her unmistakable mark in my production of "The Deluge." The play was a box-office failure, but was a herald of a new kind of theatre, freed from many of the long-accumulated barnacles of the past. It was a new and disturbing theatre experience for many who had accepted long, familiar patterns as final and wholly satisfactory.

Old adhesions are not parted with painlessly.

The bed that we make for ourselves may grow musty, but daily more comfortable. We resist eviction. It is characteristic of well-enough that it wants to be let alone.

The innovator serves a notice of eviction. He should never be surprised at lack of welcome.

Aside from the emergence of Pauline Lord, "The Deluge" marked another event, celebrated only by me, my birth as a director and the first clear interpretation of my theatre dream. This apparent failure brought me joy that has not diminished with the years.

The part of 'Sadie' in "The Deluge" was comparatively easy for Polly. 'Anna Christie' was an infinitely severer challenge.

To my mind, the bewildered, innocent prostitute is O'Neill's top character creation, a bitter, deeply compassionate indictment of a snap-judging ill-informed world.

As I have told you, Polly is not a fast-blooming plant. Her roots are deep and not quickly reached. Without their nourishment her work is lifeless, but all of the time there are notes in that haunting voice that are unmistakable soundings of the rich flow that is to come.

And then, one day, near the end of rehearsals, the flow is freed and the full promise of the soundings is revealed.

At the end of the last rehearsal of "Anna Christie," before the scenery came in, Polly threw her arms around me and wept, "That's all I can do with it." "I should hope so," I said. "Nobody could stand much more."

As I have told you, my conversion occurred in my observation of vaudeville artists. The confirmation came with occasional revelations in the legitimate theatre, and finally brought to demonstration and conviction by the production of "The Deluge."

The next step, and one of lasting and richly rewarding import, was my meeting with Robert Edmond Jones.

The angels that watch over our destinies occasionally reveal a rare gift for casting. It is not only marriages that are made in Heaven.

Irving meets Terry, and a great theatre dynasty is born.

D'Annunzio meets Duse, and two streams become a turbulent river.

John Barrymore meets Edward Sheldon, and a frivolous comedian becomes a great tragedian.

The casting angels were particularly astute when they sent Bob Jones my way, and later, when they sent John Barrymore looking for us to complete a trinity that brought to America the richest theatre period of modern time.

Out of New Hampshire chill and Harvard austerity melted a fevered, bursting young artist seeking, of all places, the theatre. He haunted the theatres of America and Europe, brooded over the work of **Gordon Craig** and Reinhardt and found himself consumed by rebellion, a rebellion not unlike the one I had been lonesomely nursing.

We both saw the theatre a better, freer, more eloquent place than anyone here or abroad was making it.

"It just isn't good enough," Bob kept protesting. "It just isn't good enough."

Stage settings in that day were largely left to the scene painter, the property man, and the electrician.

There was no general pattern, no unity, no dream.

Excesses in acting were paralleled by excesses in stage trappings.

Belasco had carried stage realism to its last offense.

Embossed letter-heads bearing the character's beautifully engraved name. Imagine!

A window in Childs, where actual butter-cakes were actually made. Imagine!

Actual spaghetti. Imagine!

Actual apple-sauce. Imagine!

A world of actuality, where the only imagination was in the breathless exclamations of adoring critics who were worshipers of pains, pains that were taken, and pains that were given.

You can see that every protest of Jones against stage settings could have been used without changing a word in my protests against accepted acting.

There was a natural fusion, which years of warm association have welded closer in aspiration and friendship.

Our first production together was a dramatization by Edith Ellis of Maxwell's "The Devil's Garden." For the first time I saw settings that heightened the impact of simplicity and honesty I was seeking, and over all, like an added blessing, a new kind of embracing beauty.

The play failed, but like "The Deluge" it was not failure to us. We knew we were on the road we had both been seeking.

Following "The Devil's Garden" was "The Happy Ending," a phantasy about war and death, by the Macphersons, with music by Eugen Haile.

Here, indeed, Jones surpassed himself. He brought a new sense of space and beauty that was exalting. The play failed, but again there were unexpected returns.

Alexander Woollcott, then critic on the Times, who had written a warm and perceptive review, telephoned, asked me to lunch.

I had never met Alec, and I was surprised that a critic would want to hobnob with the producer of a failure. That is not the New York way. This meeting was the beginning of a friendship that was warm and enduring.

Alec was much more of a person than his biographies and acid lore picture him. He was kind oftener than he was virulent, more concerned about the well faring of people he believed in than they were themselves. And above all, he had a consuming love of the theatre.

He decked it with many garlands, and made it a more beautiful and exciting place than it has been since his departure.

Another dividend of quite a different kind came from J. J. Shubert, in whose theatre "The Happy Ending" was playing to his considerable loss, as well as mine.

J. J. had a hard-boiled reputation. But the same hard-boiled man said he wanted me to have a new theatre the Shuberts were building on Forty-fifth Street. I regretted

I had no money to lease a theatre. The hard-boiled one said, "You don't need any money. Your credit is good. Take the theatre."

Out of an apparent failure came the friendship of Alec Woollcott and the Plymouth Theatre.

So you see—you never know!

Following "The Happy Ending" I chose Clare Kummer's "Good Gracious Annabelle."

Here again was a test. Could my theories of simplicity stand up with farce comedy, a kind of theatre that had been smothered with elaboration. There was only one way to find out. Jones had not learned the word compromise. His idea of the Waldorf's stuffed Peacock Alley was a shallow set, one long flat with three curtained French windows, two plain settees, two chairs, all with summer covers. Naturally, this made the best kind of screen for actors to play against.

The rich man's country garden was a back drop, and three foliage arches; no fountains, no trellises, no walks, no statuary, no obvious wealth; yet, there, by some magic, unmistakable richness.

It sounds strange to us now that these innovations seemed bold, but that is because they have been so generally accepted, until the recent unaccountable swing back to lush elaboration.

For the moment, the architect is challenging the painter.

Designers are again piling up lumber, denuding the forests as well as production budgets. This, too, shall pass.

With an able cast, including Lola Fisher, Walter Hampden, Edwin Nicander, Mae Vokes and Roland Young, a cast seizing upon new ways like escaped prisoners, "Good Gracious Annabelle" was an immediate success.

There were grumbling dissents about actors playing with their backs to the audience and a Peacock Alley that looked not in the least as everyone knew Peacock Alley to be. But these dissents dwindled into whispers in the very audible approval.

So, in a comparatively short time, I had demonstrated the soundness of my theories in drama, tragedy, comedy and phantasy, formed the invaluable association with Robert Edmond Jones, found a rare friend in Alexander Woollcott and acquired the Plymouth Theatre, that later was to reveal great achievements.

The dream had taken visible and rewarding form.


### QUESTION PERIOD

It should always be borne in mind that there are two distinct approaches to acting, subjective and objective.

Subjective acting is motivated by what is believed to be right, the actor being the servant of the character he is portraying, regardless of audience approval.

Objective acting is frankly aimed at audience approval —at what will sell.

The chief criticism of the commercial theatre is not that it is operated for profit, but that in its quest for immediate acceptance it commercializes the approach of all concerned.

It makes salesmen of dramatists, actors and directors.

The essential right of creative growth is sharply curtailed—the right to fail of approval.

The same denial in the laboratory would put an end to scientific development.

Instead of shame for unworthy work there is shame for failure to please.

There is too little shame for success won by unworthy work.

The ironic part of the commercial aim is that it is so persistently uncommercial in result. The safe way repeatedly proves the way to disaster. Bad plays cannot be made good plays by salesmanship. Promising plays are frequently robbed of their only chance by eager salesmanship.

A play that has to be sold should not be produced.

It is a mistake to blame actors for appearing in unworthy plays. Actors must work and they have seen plays for which they had little hope prove successful and, to their surprise, called worthy.

It is not to be said that objective acting is without distinction, but it is not to be confused with character creation.

Among the great of the objective actors is Al Jolson, but throughout he remains Jolson.

Contrast Jolson singing "Mammy" with Bert Williams singing "Nobody."

Williams magically disappeared in the character he created. Jolson becomes more and more Jolson, and the Mammy he yearns for is pushed farther away than Dixie.

Frank Fay is one of the most adept of the objective actors. Josephine Hull is one of theatre's few great creative artists. In the same performance, "Harvey," we have two sharply contrasting examples of wholly different ap-

proaches. One is exploitation. The other is submersion.
One is selling. The other is being.

Artistically, Miss Hull's is the true achievement.

Contrast the tireless and tiring calesthenics of Elizabeth
Bergner with the quiet authority of Ethel Barrymore.

In the past, musical comedy has been frankly objective
but now the creative artist is beginning to take over—
Gertrude Lawrence, a dream of versatility in "Lady In
The Dark"; Ethel Merman in her brilliant and uncom-
promising characterization of Annie Oakley; David
Wayne in his complete and happy surrender to the nim-
ble, engaging leprechaun in "Finian's Rainbow."

The great actors of the past knew that immersion in
the character was an adjustment that had to be made
repeatedly if the character was not to be lost.

Salvini, after he had played Othello thousands of times,
appeared at the theatre every night at six o'clock and
walked back and forth on a dark stage gathering Othello
again into his being.

Laurence Olivier, today, follows the same practice.
When he appears on the stage he is already wholly immersed in the character he is to portray. He needs no
promptings as to his identity.

Contrast this with the last minute rush of many actors
who give themselves scarcely time to apply the externals
of the character. These performances quickly fall into a
superficial stencil that with repetition becomes boring to
the actor, a boredom that cannot be concealed from the
audience.

The letter remains but the spirit has vanished.

The great adventure of acting is the abandonment of

personal identity in the creation of another character.

Character creation is a form of rebirth.

The great artists lived many lives and found renewal and expansion of being.

Theirs was not escape from life, but escape into life.

The albatross of unchanging personality dangles conspicuously from too many actors.

There is no sentence of death on the fully created character. The character lives after the creator has gone.

Peter Pan, Sadie Thompson, The Copperhead, The Music Master and a host of others are still with us though the curtain has fallen on their creators.

You ask what stage setting of recent times I consider fully expressive of the scene designer's highest function.

The only recent design that I can recommend for your study is that for "The Iceman Cometh" by Robert Edmond Jones. Here is stark, brooding simplicity that, with no loss of sordidness, evokes beauty.

The one distracting note was the sign on the door of a closet in the corner, saying, "This Is It." For hours we watched men drinking steadily, but no one ever used the door marked "This Is It." This aroused speculation that had nothing at all to do with the play, and the longer the drinkers held out the more persistent the speculation became.

The mind is errant and as inquisitive as a child about non-essentials. Even the mature mind is constantly saying, "Why, Papa, Why?"

The author, scene designer, or director should never invite such distracting meanderings while "some necessary question of the play be then to be considered."

# CHAPTER IX

# JOHN BARRYMORE

THE casting angels were especially perceptive and co-operative when they sent John Barrymore to me, and he was literally sent since I had nothing to do with his coming.

Attending a performance of "A Successful Calamity," he looked me up during an intermission, introduced himself, and said he had read I planned a production of Tolstoy's "The Living Corpse" and would like to do it with me. I told him the part was his whenever he was ready.

He had a tour of "Peter Ibbetson" to finish and said he would get in touch with me when he returned.

Those preliminaries were so brief and nebulous that I would not have been surprised at hearing no more from him. But he telephoned on his return in the Spring. We had lunch. The arrangements were completed, so you see how little I had to do with bringing about an association that was to make theatre history.

I recommend your faith in the casting angels.

Barrymore's youth had been frantic and frequently alarming.

He was a born light comedian, but in his early years the world, too, was just another comedy stage. His favorite element, on and off the stage, was hot water, from whose scaldings he blithely escaped by his own special exit, marked charm. He seemed scarcely the material for the molding of a serious artist. His talent was unmistakable, but his intentions seemed less than honorable. And then the magic transformation occurred.

He was awakened by the faith in him of Edward Sheldon, and doubtless prodded by the Mendelian genes of his gifted and determined grandmother. For years, the fabulous Mrs. Drew was the shining light of her own repertoire theatre in Philadelphia. She played with the great of her day as her visiting stars. She was the Mahomet to whom the mountains came.

It would be asking too much to expect this flaming personality to be extinguished by the mere intervention of death, so she persisted in her children, John and Georgie Drew, and then found triple emphasis in her grandchildren, Ethel, Lionel and John. From present indications, she considered that persistence enough.

But with all of Mrs. Drew's tenacity, it might have come to nothing in John's case without the intervention of, the ordinarily least persistent, Ned Sheldon.

Sheldon, a playwright of fine achievement and still greater promise, was suddenly struck by slow death, which lingered over its tardy task for more than thirty years. We are told that there are compensating replacements for physical losses.

In Sheldon's case, this hope was richly fulfilled, but the compensations were wholly spiritual. In partial death he became more vibrant and alive than he had been before sentence was pronounced upon him.

He was the guide and counselor of stars and dramatists who came to him seeking inspiration and renewed faith.

He was the first to hear the plans of stars and the latest works of dramatists. His interest, concern and enthusiasm never wavered. He kept in touch with all that his friends were doing and contemplating.

Blind and stricken, he was more alive than his visitors, who left him feeling themselves the handicapped and poor in spirit.

Before he was laid low, Sheldon had put the finger of destiny on John Barrymore. He foresaw all that he was to become. His determination for Jack never wavered. He made plans far into the future. Barrymore was to be the great Hamlet.

If you knew the Jack of that day, you would realize the boldness of the forecast. With all of Jack's talents, he scarcely had the voice for poetic roles. There was a rasp that was not easily set to music. But Sheldon could hear the music. The blind hear sounds that do not register on normal ears.

Either through Sheldon's, or her own perception, Emilie Hapgood, too, saw Barrymore's potentials. Together they persuaded Jack to play Falder in Galsworthy's "Justice."

With this, the great flight began.

Barrymore was at once revealed as a serious artist of great promise. Whatever misgivings he, himself, may have had were dissipated. A new day had come, the bright day that Sheldon had foretold.

Following "Justice," Jack played "Peter Ibbetson," with Lionel asserting his new aspirations in an incomparable portrait of Colonel Ibbetson.

In "Ibbetson" Jack first revealed the sensitive, poetic artist with the translucence of the dreams in which he moved, this, in spite of a voice that had not yet been freed.

I am taking you on this ascent of an artist to the unfamiliar heights in the hope that you may find a pinnacle from which the unexplored comes into clearer view.

Rehearsals for "The Living Corpse," now called "Redemption," began with the usual reading which, to my surprise, revealed Barrymore employing a newly acquired Russian accent. I stopped the reading early and dismissed the company for lunch. As we sat down to lunch, Jack, who had an uncanny sense of disapproval, asked, "What's the matter?"

"It's the accent," I replied. "You are a Russian among Russians, all of you speaking Russian. An accent makes you seem a foreigner among your own people."

While he saw the incongruity, the attempt was heartening. Without saying anything about it, he had spent weeks with a White Russian acquiring an authentic aristocratic accent.

This painstaking determination to be authentic was characteristic of a normally unindustrious man that he never abandoned.

In every way, he was the hardest working actor I have known.

Nothing was too much trouble.

He would make endless trips to costumers, shoe-makers and wig-makers.

When we were later doing "Richard III," Bob Jones wanted special armor made for Richard. We located a former armorer running a machine shop in Newark. He agreed to work with us. In those days Newark was not so easily reached, but Jack made countless trips to Newark to make sure that the armor was right.

It was not the excess pains he took that counted, but the clear evidence of his complete dedication.

He was at rehearsal first.

He knew his part first.

In the days of preparation nothing else was allowed a moment's attention, day or night.

Always bear in mind that this was the irresponsible, shiftless Jack Barrymore, whose infractions and indifferences had been the despair of stage managers for years.

Unlike Ethel and Lionel, with whom I was to work later, Jack was quick to unfold. Each day's rehearsal revealed the wider range of his exploration.

It was like watching the working of a treasure mine and occasionally, as director, detecting and revealing to him treasure that he was overlooking. All of my criticism of his work was based on his own best examples.

"You are not bringing to this scene the penetration that you reveal in the previous scenes. If you show your best at any time, you are obliged to show your best all the time. Otherwise, you bring proof against yourself. Your fair will never stand up against your best."

You will see that in this process I never attempted to give Barrymore anything that was not his own. I was a weighing machine revealing to him when his delivery was short or overweight. It was rarely short, but frequently overweight.

Despite his humor, usually a safeguard against exaggeration, there was in Jack a residue of the old bombastic theatre, the theatre that Grandmother Drew had long made her own.

We never entered into long dissections of meanings.

There was nothing of the Stanislawsky fabrication of antecedent life or unrevealed influence.

We found full guidance in what Tolstoy had clearly pictured.

The most immediately corrective criticism of Jack was the suggestion that he reminded me, for a moment, of some actor whose work he particularly despised. There was quite a list of these, and in them a fairly complete catalogue of all the offenses against intelligent theatre.

This is a way of correction I have frequently used with other actors, and for effectiveness I recommend it to you. An actor, holding up the mirror to nature, does not like to be confronted by a visage that he has never admired. You will find numerous undesirable models in public life and literature, which you can use to good advantage.

There are many goblins that will get actors if they don't watch out. Goblins are just as effective in promoting good behavior in the theatre as in the nursery. So do not hesitate to make use of them.

We had a good company in "Redemption," and rehearsals proceeded without confusion, an experience new to Barrymore.

Occasionally he had misgivings over the absence of familiar theatrical supports, but there was something in the atmosphere of certainty that reassured him.

You will find that if, as director, you convey the sense of knowing exactly where you are going, you will not have many worried inquiries on the way. Before long, Jack's misgiving disappeared. He was having a friendlier climate for the planting and tending of his garden than he had previously experienced. There were no level-ing storms of disagreement, no blights of fear or doubt, no drouth of doom.

All that was conducive to Jack's rich blooming was there, and before rehearsals were over his garden was in rich, full flower.

The director never plants the seed.

The seed is in all of us at birth.

The director cannot be the gardener, for each man must tend his own garden if he is to bring forth the prod-ucts of his own seed. Only he has access to it.

At best, the director is a horticultural expert who understands the conditions most favorable for the gar-den's release of the energy that is in the seed.

Above all, the director must be careful not to trample the garden and destroy the seed.

The director's reward and joy are as escort of new creation and as bearer of good tidings.

"How beautiful on the mountain are the feet of him that bringeth good tidings."

The production for "Redemption" was, of course, de-signed by Robert Edmond Jones. Here was a blending of simplicity, beauty and doom, settings that spoke without comment; backgrounds that understood the tortured Fedya and the pathetic little world he shattered while shattering himself.

As a perfect example of lint picking that should carry you through the rest of the Summer, I bring you the gem of my collection. As with subsequent productions with Jack, we were opening at the Plymouth with no out-of-town preliminaries. We gave full performances with no audience.

Out of gratitude to Tolstoy, whom I had no way of thanking, I invited his son, Count Tolstoy, to a performance given wholly in his honor. He was to be the only guest and witness. There was no publicity. It had all the aspects of a royal command performance with only the king in attendance.

Jack surpassed himself that night, and the cast stayed right with him. It was the most impressive performance I had ever shared up to that time. Feeling certain that I would find Tolstoy consumed with the experience and its attendant memories, I went to the Count after the final curtain.

He fixed a cold and outraged eye on me, and demanded: "Where is Fedya's beard?"

Nothing that Barrymore had done could offset the outrage of a Fedya without a beard.

So you see, a bit of lint can be a mighty mote in the eye that sees little.

"Redemption" opened, and with it a new era. Overnight several rings were added to the American theatre oak. Jack surpassed the seeming perfection of his final dress performance. There was no sign of first-night nerves, no indication of consciousness of challenge.

He really took the stage. His authority was unmistakable.

Here were the hidden miracles of creation taking clear form for all to see. Everyone knew that something vital and disturbing was happening.

Not all were sure that they liked it. Some found it a needless dwelling on agony and defeat. The notices, while full of praise, conveyed a sense of Russian brooding and doom. They were the kind of good notices that con-

vey a warning. For several weeks the warning was heeded.
Our fate was in heavy doubt.

Now, in my brief business talk with Barrymore, I told
him that it was my plan to have him stay at the Plymouth
for three years, and to make that possible we would have
other plays planned to follow "Redemption."

To Jack, this seemed expecting a good deal—three
years. As it developed, we could easily have stayed ten
years, or for that matter, for the rest of his life.

To have this dream shattered by a failure of "Redemption" so sudden that there would be no time to prepare
another play was a prospect not to be considered, so we
just did not consider it. We had to have faith and wait.

Fortunately, I was in my own theatre and could not be
closed by a contract stop clause. Night after night I
watched small audiences being transported by the play.
They found none of the gloom that had disturbed first-
nighters, but a new kind of exaltation.

I knew that every night we were turning out a few
hundred volunteer press agents, whose enthusiasm must
finally tell. The suspense hung over us until the fifth
week, and then the tide took a sudden turn. Soon we were
selling out, and we continued selling out until the
thirtieth week, when, though still turning people away,
I closed "Redemption" to make way for "The Jest."

Thus, we were adhering to the original plan to present
a series of plays.

With the survival of "Redemption" beyond the first
poor weeks, we had looked upon the last empty seat we
were to see in the nearly three years of the Barrymore en-
gagement that followed. Only faintness of heart could
have defeated us.

More than once I have had reason to be thankful for my heritage of Welsh stubbornness.

I urge upon you the value of stubbornness in the theatre. There are times it is the only rock on which you can stand. If you abandon it, you will be engulfed.

Be stubborn—and have faith.

## QUESTION PERIOD

I am afraid the point I wanted to emphasize in yesterday's paper did not emerge. The salient point that may be of value to you in the future is that temporary failure may be the road to ultimate success.

No matter what the outcome of a production, if it is a step toward the goal you are seeking, it cannot be classified as a failure. More properly may failure be attributed to a success in which there is no advance.

It was the impression that a failure, "The Happy Ending" made on J. J. Shubert that put me in possession of the Plymouth Theatre. But for that possession, the Barrymore series might have come to a sudden end at its beginning.

We are not always accurate in classifying our blessings. If you are on the right track, forces that you know nothing about come to your aid. It is characteristic of the dream that its fulfillment far surpasses it.

Henry Ford, dreaming of a small cheaply constructed, cheaply operated motor to be attached to a buggy, saw his dream expand into a vast new era; likewise Edison, Marconi and the first makers of pictures that flickered.

So with the dreamers of a new country that would, one day, stretch to the far Mississippi.

**Ideas** find their own ways of fulfillment.

If you pursue the dream of a better theatre, unexpected help will come to you as it repeatedly came to me.

While I was dreaming, Edward Sheldon was working. The true director of John Barrymore's rich career was Edward Sheldon. It was Sheldon who took Barrymore up to the high mountain.

Now there is direction at its best, revealing to the actor his own unused potentials and awakening in him a desire to bring them into being.

It was Sheldon who sent Barrymore to me to do "Redemption." It was Sheldon who advised us to follow "Redemption" with "The Jest." It was Sheldon who made the brilliant adaptation of "The Jest," the most unforgettable poetic melodrama of modern times. It was Sheldon who would take neither credit nor royalty for his work, a work that he knew he would never even see or hear.

Sheldon, lying helpless, only a few city blocks away, never witnessed any of the high achievements for which he was responsible, yet no one drew as much joy from them as he.

If joy in complete detachment from self and devotion to enriching the lives of others is the mark of the saint, Edward Sheldon was canonized by his own life.

What all actors can learn from Barrymore is that his fulfillment came when he abandoned the externals of acting in the use of which he had been expert and successful.

With this severance he made way for creative sources long dormant within him and, for the most part, dormant in all of us.

In the early days the Mormons established one of the first repertoire theatres in America. It was their custom to begin each rehearsal with prayer. This may have been mere formality, or it may have been their realization that truly creative work is an expression of God. To them "Thy will be done" may not have been resignation but affirmation.

# CHAPTER X

# JOHN, ETHEL AND LIONEL

It was in "The Jest" I first worked with Lionel Barrymore. He had just finished playing the aged Milt Shanks in "The Copperhead." And when he came to the first rehearsal he was still Milt Shanks, a bent, old man. Beyond any actor I have known, Lionel became imprisoned in the character he was playing.

Milt Shanks seemed hardly a likely candidate for the blustering, violent Neri, the ruthless mercenary.

And then, at the end of two weeks' rehearsal, Milt Shanks disappeared. In his place stood the towering, jeering, terrifying Neri. This was not something externally applied. It was an inner conflagration, a kind of self-hypnosis. I was to learn later that all of his performances had a trance-like quality. He seemed wholly unaware of anything but the experience he was living. There was no audience. He was caught in the dream that was no part of his surroundings. There was a complete immersion in what he was doing that we see only in dreams.

I do not know how many of you have ever observed your dreams. I advise you to cultivate the habit, for only there will you see perfect acting. No one ever makes a wrong move. Whatever dream characters do is inevitable.

Observe particularly groups or crowds, how completely

individual they remain, and yet how wholly they merge into a mass entity. As for individual and varied facial expressions and bodily responses, those we can never hope to duplicate.

There is a close relationship between the dream and make-believe. At its best, the theatre is an invoked dream, a mass dream experienced by people aware and awake, but transported out of reality.

It is what happens to a roaring crowd of baseball fans. With the dream state removed, baseball would become a dull business. Observe the preliminary infield practice, the beautiful co-ordination of mind and body, the ball being rifled about with such speed that it seems a magic messenger touching heavy footed man into electric movements of agility and beauty. There is no more beautiful ballet than the expert infield practice of a professional baseball team.

Baseball is much more than a contest. It takes on a dream quality, of which the spectator becomes part. He, too, is free and dancing, easily retrieving difficult throws, and with no break in rhythm speeding the messenger on its way.

Certainly the worshiping crowds who screamed with joy in the presence of Hitler were caught up in a dream, a nightmare in which they were transported participants.

But deepest of all in the nightmare was Hitler, himself. One had only to listen to one of his speeches to know that he was a man possessed. His demon screamed and spewed its hatred.

Now, in the best sense, the actor who creates the dream is himself caught up in the dream. The dream becomes his reality.

One had only to be in Duse's presence to know that she moved in a region created by forces of which she was the instrument.

The same was true of Moissi.

And Isadora Duncan.

And startlingly true of Lionel Barrymore.

This very quality made him a frightening figure in "Macbeth," a figure too possessed for the comfort of his audiences.

It is ironic that a character whose evil possession is foretold by the witches should be rejected because of the actor's relentless revealing of that evil possession.

After "Macbeth," I produced Henri Bernstein's "The Claw," with Lionel. Here was the picture of an aging statesman caught in the fatal quest of second romantic youth. Somehow, disintegration brought on by passion, is a possession more readily accepted than possession by the evil forces of the world. So "Macbeth" failed, and "The Claw" was a great success.

But with the failure of "Macbeth," the lure of the theatre had disappeared, and Lionel soon became comfortably embalmed in celluloid.

I have often been asked to compare Jack and Lionel.

Jack believed that Lionel was the greatest actor of his time.

Lionel believed that Jack was the most commanding and gifted presence in the theatre that we are likely to behold. My feeling is that both were right.

Following "The Jest" was "Richard III." Here was the beginning of the great adventure that was to lead to "Hamlet." And here again the casting angels stepped in. Jack had all the beauties except voice.

The final beauty was contributed by Margaret Carrington, a retired opera singer, who had developed a method of her own of voice perfection. She was deeply interested in the theatre, and deplored the vocal offenses too prevalent on the stage.

Here again, Jack demonstrated his determination to pursue perfection. The Jack of an earlier day would have thought voice instruction a hilarious idea. But the day of levity had passed. If Mrs. Carrington had a secret he wanted it.

So he labored for long days with an instructor who was no easy taskmaster. Mrs. Carrington had the kind of derision that Jack appreciated. He took her most merciless barbs and went back for more.

To her, he was the great opportunity that she long had sought.

Just to find one voice that was really worth freeing, to hear just once the grandeur of Shakespeare's lines with unobstructed accompaniment. So, after long perseverance, two dreams were realized—Mrs. Carrington's and Jack's.

In the meantime, production plans were being made far ahead. Robert Edmond Jones had planned a brooding setting, with London Tower in the background. Against this towering background that was to dwarf the people, all scenes were played—processions, battle scenes, love scenes, death scenes.

Jones spent months in England collecting fabrics and armor, and Jack was shuttling between armorers, costumers and Mrs. Carrington.

There was great skepticism about Jack attempting Shakespeare. There was also anxious anticipation. With

Jack's first soliloquy, all doubts were removed. A glorious voice read glorious words as they had never been heard before.

The young prince had come into his kingdom.

Once more, Jack's first performance was his best.

In a brief four weeks our triumph was brought to a sudden end. Jack was the victim of a serious breakdown. He wanted to go on, but I insisted on his closing. There was little advance sign of this catastrophe. There was a mistaken impression that he had been dissipating, but never at any time while he was with me did he dissipate. This was doubtless the first warning of the complete and tragic collapse that was ultimately to overtake him.

I had planned to follow "Richard III" with "Lilion," "Cyrano" and "Hamlet." But now our great adventure was to be halted for two years, and finally to be ended with our production of "Hamlet."

In the meantime, I had begun a series of productions with Ethel Barrymore, starting with Hauptman's "Rose Bernd." Ethel Barrymore, at that time, possessed neither Jack's determination nor Lionel's earnest submersion. She had worked much longer and harder than either of them. Success had come to her early, and it was essentially the success of a radiant, beautiful person with a golden, unforgettable voice.

In contrast to Jack, her first performance was her worst, and in contrast to Lionel she was, at all times, acutely conscious of all that was happening about her. As a person, she had greater depth than either. She was the unselfish Barrymore at all times, more concerned about her brothers than herself.

Though her devotion brought scant appreciation,

nothing could alter her faith in their importance as important artists, or her love of them as endearing, endlessly amusing people.

We followed "Rose Bernd" with "Romeo and Juliet," which I made the mistake of opening in New York without preliminary performances. This was followed with Sutro's "The Laughing Lady" and "The Second Mrs. Tanqueray," both of which were successful.

Two years ago I produced a revival of Philip Barry's "The Joyous Season," in which Ethel gave the rarest performance of her later years. We were playing in Philadelphia. After the first act, a woman looked me up, and said to me:

"Do you know how I feel when that woman comes on the stage?"

"No."

"I feel that we should all stand up."

That is a revealing summary of Ethel Barrymore's effect on audiences.

She is in the truest sense a presence. Even before she has spoken, an audience realizes with her appearance that something has happened, that the air is charged with new power. Even her shadow on the screen does not lose that impact. She is the last of a long line of great theatre personalities. She is the final recapitulation of a grand tradition.

At last, John Barrymore returned to do "Hamlet."

To my mind, this was the great and crowning achievement of the modern theatre. Never was one man more blessed with all of the attributes of the complex, towering, haunting Dane—beauty, grace, eloquence, humor, pathos and power.

How the last words of Horatio regretfully reminded us: "We shall not look upon his like again."

As in the preceding plays, Jack's first performance was his best, and thereafter his interest waned.

To him, the curse of the theatre was repetition.

The enthusiasms of audiences did not revive him.

Some of his performances were bad, not from indifference, but from over-playing.

He seemed to be forcing himself into a frenzy of interest that he no longer felt.

An inner quarrel was being forced into outer view.

He knew that the theatre world was his, and he knew that he ought to want it, but his sickened heart was not in it.

Perhaps "Hamlet" should not have been done so soon. After "Hamlet"—what? He faced the Alexandrian dilemma. What new world was there to be conquered?

His theater flights were like the nuptial flight of the bee—a glorious ascent into high, rarefied air, momentary exaltation and then quick death.

It is a mistake to think that Barrymore left the theatre for Hollywood money. His theatre earnings were much more than he wanted or could use. His short nine weeks' road tour of "Hamlet" netted him over Fifty Thousand Dollars.

The lure of Hollywood was the absence of repetition. Once a picture was finished, succeeding performances were neatly wrapped in cans. He could fish in the Southern Pacific while he was appearing throughout the world.

From my last meeting with him, some time before his death, I knew that he had condemned and sentenced himself for what he had abandoned. I realized that his willingness to exhibit himself as a ridiculous figure in radio, and finally on the stage, was self castigation. He needed no one to reproach him.

If there is a final accounting, he had his ruthlessly drawn up. There would be no condemnation he had not already anticipated. It is tragic to stand helplessly while a man destroys himself, but even more tragic to see the divine flame abandoned at the height of its incandescence.

High achievement is not measured by length of duration. The Great lives from Jesus to Lincoln had comparatively brief periods of realization. It would be a mistake to conclude that because of later disintegration, John Barrymore was a failure. Nothing subsequent to his great creative era could destroy his rich period of full realization.

He charted new areas of expression that remain open for others to explore. Where man has been, man will go again. Areas once visited do not remain content with neglect.

We speak of beckoning stars, beckoning winds, beckoning tides, beckoning lands. There are similarly vast regions of beckoning in the souls of men.

These regions, once visited, will beckon again.

They, too, are in need of fulfillment.

There is a law of demand and supply which operates in the world of spirit.

Demands that have been set up by achievements of Barrymore will not rest because he is no longer here to meet them. These demands will create their own supply.

There are liberators of the spirit.

In our theatre time John Barrymore was the greatest

of these. The liberator not only frees his own time, he frees succeeding time. The area that knew Barrymore will know him again in the persons of others.

Such a man's obituary is never completed.

New chapters are written by those who follow him.

Failure indeed! John Barrymore was success of the highest lustre.

He is one of the beckoning stars, and in the galaxy with him is Edward Sheldon, his own beckoning star.

Long may they shine together.

## QUESTION PERIOD

Yes, all of the Barrymore productions were designed by Robert Edmond Jones, as well as those of a number of others produced by me.

From the beginning, Jones and I had the same approach to all productions, the chief guides of which are simplicity and authority.

Jones as designer, and I as director, agreed at all times that our contributions should not be individual, but supporting parts of the whole pattern. This resulted in a harmony of background and action otherwise unattainable.

After the movement of the play had been set, Jones sat through rehearsals to check his work with mine and to plan his light plots in relation to the arranged positions.

Thus, before a production was set up, it had been completely envisioned by both of us so that the arrival of the scenery, costumes and properties rarely revealed a problem which we had not foreseen.

This greatly simplified that difficult transition from the bare stage rehearsals to the finished production, a transition which frequently has lost the perfection of performance on a bare stage—a perfection never to be recovered.

If confusion develops with the introduction of the physical production it puts an emphasis on accessories which tends to rob performances of their ease and spontaneity. Values lost in long, tiring, badly planned dress rehearsals are not easily recovered. It is something like the dislike a woman takes to a dreamed-of gown that has been poorly executed for first fitting. No amount of alteration can quite restore her original certainty.

In the past, bad dress rehearsals were taken for granted. The surprise that anything that seemed so bad could eventually be made even nearly right probably led to the old superstition that a bad dress rehearsal is a good omen. On that basis there should be almost no failures.

In modern plays it is important that the author and director should agree as to how the physical production is to be treated. If one thinks of it in simple, imaginative terms and the other in elaborate, realistic terms, these are obviously ends that no scene designer can meet. Nor should the scene designer be expected to assume responsibility for a production unless he knows what the general approach is to be.

Collaboration in actual production begins at this point and should not wait for the designer's first sketches based on manuscript descriptions which are at variance with what the author and director have finally agreed upon.

In this, as in all other phases of production, it is important for the director to know what he wants.

The designer can, and usually does, surpass the director's conception by heightening the intent.

What the director has stumblingly tried to say, the designer says in clear and eloquent terms. The designer is much like the professional letter writer who composes beautiful missives for the unpoetic swain.

In planning, the director is important to the designer, but in execution the designer must have a free hand.

If you are fortunate to work with a Robert Edmond Jones in your future productions, you will know that the casting angels are with you.

Without him theatre life would have been much less shining for me and many others.

# CHAPTER XI

# FLASHES OF GENIUS

BY THIS time I am sure you know that I believe the only theatre expression of lasting value is creative. In the theatre, as in all other arts, the preponderance of expression is imitative. This is not strange since from the beginning imitation has been man's chief road to learning and usefulness.

Birds, animals and children learn by imitation. Through ages of imitation a pattern is so embedded that it becomes a part of the common heritage.

But there is no imitation of creative work that has the pulse of the original. The kindling breath is absent.

Mark Twain was an inveterate buyer of new gadgets. While living in Hartford he was one of the first subscribers to that new gadget, the telephone.

Now, Twain had managed to conceal from Mrs. Twain the fact that in her absence he exercised his magnificent repertoire of profanity, gathered from these most eloquent cursers, the Mississippi River pilots. The telephone service of that early day did little to discourage profanity.

On one occasion, when Twain was particularly exasperated by the failure of the gadget, he burned the balky wires with his richest river invective. Hanging up with a grand flourish, he turned and, to his surprise, saw the cold-faced Mrs. Twain.

Perhaps Mrs. Twain had been taught by her mother that the way to cure a husband of profanity was to join him in the pastime. At any rate, in rather halting words, she repeated Twain's telephone comments. Twain looking at her admiringly, but rather regretfully, said,

"My dear you have the words, but not the music."

That is apt criticism of much of the acting today.

Actors say the words, but the music of illumination is missing. Words are ladled from the surface of the actor's mind. They are not brought to new life and new meaning by having passed through the actor's inner fire.

The actor's mind is working, but not his heart.

We find the same lack in public speaking.

Contrast the usual public speech with one by Winston Churchill. The magic quality which Churchill exhorted from familiar words held an empire together. There was no greater castigation of Hitler than Churchill's simple description "That Evil Man."

How much more powerful than the familiar screams of "Murderer," "Destroyer," "Ravager." These carried the hysteria of common slander.

But the words, "That Evil Man," as spoken by Churchill, were condemnation with the finality of St. Peter.

They robbed the accused of all defense. In war there is easily claimed justification for murder and destruction. They are the essentials of war. But in war or peace there is no appeal from the verdict as pronounced by Churchill, "That Evil Man."

It is possible that Churchill's condemnation contributed more to Hitler's hysterical disintegration and resultant mad decisions than all the guns that were turned against him.

The man who had destroyed his people by the mad use of words himself destroyed by their deeper, calmer, deadlier use.

Words to live again must be given a transfusion of inner emotion. It is not speech that grips us in the theatre, but impact. Sometimes three or four words will turn us over with the force of an avalanche.

I remember impatiently sitting through two dull acts of "The Women," a sorry collection of artificial, acidulous characters skating on the thin ice of useless existence, when a child learning that her mother is about to apply for divorce cries out in horror:

"Mother, you can't do it! You can't do it!"

Suddenly all the artificialities disappeared, and a lost child stood alone, tragic symbol of the great army of inflicted children whose lives had been torn from a trusted and needful pattern by the selfishness of divorce.

A meaningless play took on lasting and unforgettable meaning by one little speech given unbearable impact by a child.

When Malcolm Kean played Claudius with John Barrymore in London, one cry of two words had the galvanizing impact of pure horror. Dashing from the performance of the players, the terror-stricken Claudius cried out, "Lights! Lights!" with a frenzied horror of revealed guilt that the actual murder could not have conjured.

We had all heard "Lights! Lights!" cried many times before, but never with approaching revelation.

Here was man seeing his perfidy and self violation for the first time. The frightening darkness he sought to escape had enveloped him forever. He was frantically trying to climb the glass walls of Hell.

Again the petrifying spell was cast by Moissi in "The Living Corpse."

Fedya had finished his suicide note to his wife. Now, all of his problems had vanished. At last he had found peace. He faced a small mirror on the wall, drew out a gun and raised it to his temple. There was a moment's pause, as if of farewell, then his body stiffened, the pistol was slowly lowered. He stared at the reflection, and then in surprise and horror, said, "Ich kann nicht. Ich kann nicht."

There was no fear or cowardice in the cry, just complete, incalculable defeat. These could be truly called Fedya's last words, for through the rest of the play he wanders a ghost, a living corpse.

Note, too, the art of Tolstoy in giving Fedya no more to say than "Ich kann nicht." What more could be said? A man with ready death in his hand was sentenced to life, forbidden by some unknown sentinel of his soul to step beyond that forbidden line.

In the first act of "Anna Christie," when Anna, in the back room of the saloon, is telling Marthy the reverses that ended in prostitution, says, "Then I got sick and was sent to the hospital." In Miss Lord's reading was the clear revelation of the nature of her sickness. There for all to recognize was the defiling penalty of prostitution.

In all of these instances you will see the power of words that are not said.

In Molnar's "Heavenly And Earthly Love," which I produced as "Launzi," Miss Lord as Launzi, the sensitive child, whose first love is violated by her mother, whom she worships. Such perfidy is beyond endurance. The desperate child throws herself into the river, but is frustrated by rescue.

Later, she persists in her determination. There is one friend she must seek for comfort. She cries, "I'll complain to Jesus." Those words, as the tortured Miss Lord uttered them, can never be forgotten.

What a mingling of faith and hope, of despair and death, was in those simple words, "I'll complain to Jesus."

Again the author and the artist combined to give words such meaning as they never had before.

Ethel Barrymore's famous reading of the line, "That's all there is— There isn't any more" still rings in many minds after countless intervening theatre experiences have been forgotten.

Louis Wolheim, as Captain Flagg in "What Price Glory," just back from gruelling nights and days, is ordered out again before having time to lie down. Struggling to his feet, his only comment is, "God almighty, I'm tired."

In that tired voice the weary stupidity of war was unforgettably etched.

Again, there are bits of business that conjure a picture that remains with us always.

Laurette Taylor, in "The Glass Menagerie," recalling the days when she was a Dixie belle, lifting above her ankle the skirt of her pathetic finery, waiting for the first step of the minuet.

The drab room is transformed. Candles flicker, glass

pendants glisten, the music floats through the honey-suckle air, gallants, long dead, bow before the trans-formed ruin—all summoned by the dainty lifting of a skirt.

Elsa Lehmann, the great German character actress, as the bewildered, stupid servant girl in Hauptman's "Rose Bernd." She is confessing to the invalid mistress that she is with child by the master.

In her turmoil she rubs a bursting head with a hat on it; shoves her hand under the poor millinery and rubs her head, bobbing the hat up and down. It is a picture of utter distraction, too tragic to bear.

These sudden, revealing flashes in readings and action are evidence of the creative treasure that is buried in all of us.

We are told that if we knock, the door will be opened to us.

Not only do we not knock, but we do not listen.

That inner door has two sides.

There are creative forces in the other side that seek release.

There is knocking on the other side of the door that we do not hear.

Our external ears are so occupied with outside noises that inner hearing is cut off.

The genius hears the knocking on the other side of the door.

And because he listens, the door opens to him.

He becomes the heir to the riches of inspiration.

He fulfills his reason for being.

For some reason not revealed to us, God has chosen

to create through man. Why God depends upon us for anything so important as creation is puzzling.

However, it is a distinction that man would be foolish to question. It is the one distinction that raises him above the animals.

While no man can create, every man can be God's co-creator.

Now it is not God's way to delegate responsibility without providing ample ways of fulfillment.

We can see all about us that the most extravagant hand is God's.

Millions of seeds are provided for the survival of one plant, or of one human.

Millions of men are provided for the emergence of one man who will carry Creation's plans one step farther.

And so man, at birth, is provided with many seeds, some of which he may develop, or all of which he may neglect.

Jung, in his theory of racial memory, believes that all men carry within them a record of all emotional experiences that have been accumulated by mankind from the beginning.

It is compared to the biologist's demonstration that the forming child goes through the major steps of physical evolution in a brief recapitulation of nine months.

Now, if all men are similar living emotional records, it follows that when an artist finds access to that record and brings the result into view, its authenticity will be confirmed by others, since it is part of themselves that is being revealed.

And there you have the mission of the artist.

And there you have the explanation of the reverence in which artists have long been held.

In a true sense they have found God.

They have become His co-creators.

Dr. George Washington Carver believed that of himself he was nothing. Only as an instrument of God could he have any meaning.

To Dr. Carver, God was the only Creator, the only source, the only means.

So. Dr. Carver talked to God.

When confronted by a laboratory problem, for which there seemed no solution, it was his custom to say:

"Well, Lord, I don't know what to do about this. I have to turn it over to you. You got me into this, Lord. Now You'll have to get me out."

He believed, and the answer came, over and over the answer came.

Jung's racial theory is of particular value to the dramatist, actor and director.

If within us there is a full library of human experience, what better source can we seek?

How do we find it?

By faith like Dr. Carver's?

Seek and ye shall find.

Faith, contemplation, prayer, withdrawal, believing only in inner revelation, knowing that nine-tenths of man is submerged, knowing that the submerged man always seeks externalization and, denied, will seek escape in dreams, sleeping or waking.

Listen to your waking dreams.

Encourage your aspirations.

Do not dismiss them as unattainable.

What creation seeks, it has provided for.

It has made no exception of you.

Being an author, or an actor, or a director is much more than any of these.

These are ways of fulfilling our reason for being.